The Murder Mystique

RECOGNITIONS

detective/suspense

Bruce Cassiday, General Editor

Raymond Chandler by Jerry Speir
P. D. James by Norma Siebenheller
John D. MacDonald by David Geherin
Ross Macdonald by Jerry Speir
The Murder Mystique: Crime Writers on Their Art
edited by Lucy Freeman
Dorothy L. Sayers by Dawson Gaillard
Sons of Sam Spade: The Private Eye Novel in the 70s
by David Geherin

science fiction/fantasy

Sharon Jarvis, General Editor

Isaac Asimov by Jean Fiedler and Jim Mele
Ray Bradbury by Wayne L. Johnson
Critical Encounters: Writers and Themes in Science Fiction, edited
by Dick Riley
Critical Encounters II: Writers and Themes in Science Fiction,
edited by Tom Staicar
The Feminine Eye: Science Fiction and the Women Who Write It,
edited by Tom Staicar
Frank Herbert by Timothy O'Reilly
Ursula K. LeGuin by Barbara J. Bucknall
Theodore Sturgeon by Lucy Menger

Also of Interest

The Bedside, Bathtub & Armchair Companion to Agatha Christie,
edited by Dick Riley and Pam McAllister
Introduction by Julian Symons

The Murder Mystique
Crime Writers on Their Art

Edited by
Lucy Freeman

Frederick Ungar Publishing Co.
NEW YORK

Copyright © 1982 by Frederick Ungar Publishing Co., Inc.

Printed in the United States of America

Design by Anita Duncan

Library of Congress Cataloging in Publication Data
Main entry under title:

The Murder mystique.

(Recognitions)
1. Detective and mystery stories—History and
criticism—Addresses, essays, lectures. 2. Detective
and mystery stories—Technique—Addresses, essays,
lectures. I. Freeman, Lucy. II. Series.
PN3448.D4M83   1982   809.3'872   82-40259
ISBN 0-8044-2212-5
ISBN 0-8044-6162-7 (pbk.)

Contents

Clues for the Reader

This book is for all readers who delight in mysteries—private eye novels, police procedurals, the amateur detective, the spy thriller, the locked-room puzzle—the various types that give us so many hours of suspense and pleasure. Here the crime writers themselves talk about their craft and their experiences in an area of the publishing field in which they are experts. And these are all experts—working members of the Mystery Writers of America. The book, though, has no official ties to that organization; all the writers are here on their own.

The lively discussions fall into two sections that should entertain and enlighten both readers and aspiring writers of mysteries. Or writers of any kind. I doubt I would ever have become a writer had I not developed a passion for mysteries when I was eleven. Luckily there was a library directly behind our house, and I consumed every mystery on the shelves, for adolescents and adults. I decided then and there to be a writer and give others the pleasure I had received.

The first section of this book describes the rise of the mystery, examines the various types of mystery fiction, and also true crime. The second section shows the writer at work as he (and she) offers sensitive and significant comments on technique and motivation.

Mysteries today star on the list of bestsellers. Seven of the top fifteen of 1980 were "mainstream" suspense, including Ken Follett's *The Key to Rebecca*, Robert Ludlum's *The Bourne Identity*, and Stephen King's *Firestarter*. Mysteries, if they are what publishers and agents call big books, meaning more than 500 pages, with complicated plots and complex characters, can earn as much as a popular novel about duplicity in Washington, D.C., or an exposé of the secret sex life of a Hollywood star.

In his review of the history of the mystery, Bruce Cassiday describes how it started in the mainstream with Charles Dickens. In *Bleak House*, Dickens introduced Inspector Bucket of the Detective, as he called himself. The Inspector solved a murder, after a chase through a blinding snowstorm (does anything *ever* change?). This was followed by Wilkie Collins's famous *The Moonstone* and Edward Bulwer Lytton's novels, one of which fictionalized a contemporary murder case.

Along the way to success, the mystery story became fragmented, dividing into categories such as Gothic, spy, police procedural, private eye, black detective, Jewish detective, Chinese detective, blind detective, child detective, even dog detective for children, as Helen Wells points out in her essay on juvenile mysteries, which are reaching a new high in sales for all age categories.

Today we are also seeing the paperback original, which Franklin Bandy prefers calling "softcover," in contrast to "hardcover." He tells why this new type of publishing has occurred and what the advantages are of an original softcover sale over hardcover.

The spy story, starting with John Le Carré's man who came in out of the cold, has been a hot winner. Ken Follett, who now has homes in both New York and England, explains what he considers the essential of a powerful spy story—characterization. Readers (and writers) will be intrigued by the examples of how an author develops this.

A variety of popular sleuths are also described in the following pages. Thomas Chastain writes of the private eye in the tradition of Sam Spade and Philip Marlowe. Hillary Waugh tells us about the "human rather than superhuman sleuth," the detective who is part of the official system in the police procedural novel.

How a writer transforms fact into fiction using a real murder, but giving it the special magic that makes it a bestseller, is spelled out by Shannon OCork in her inimitable style. She also offers sound advice on how to achieve style in writing by eliminating unnecessary verbiage and using taut, dramatic format that insures holding the reader with every word.

From Edward D. Hoch, noted for the number of his short stories that have been made into television and movie films, we learn of the disillusionment a writer may face when others indulge in the adapting of his written words into images. More often than not, Hoch says, the writer sees on the screen something far removed from what he has written and watches the images as if they were the work of a stranger— "as indeed they are," he concludes.

Eleanor Sullivan, editor of *Ellery Queen's Mystery Magazine* and author of short stories and film scripts, gives us a glimpse of life behind the scenes with writers. She has been fascinated by what inspires men and women to write. One famous author calls his need to write "a maternal thing," a wish to make life more acceptable. Another says writers are "the great pretenders of all time." A third: "Any art is contrived: the degree of artistry lies in how you conceal that contrivance."

Combining the professions of editor and writer, D. R. Bensen introduces a challenging concept as he discusses writing on two different levels and the conflict this creates in the writer. One is the hackwork some authors turn out for the large number of readers who do not care about artistry in writing, wanting only to enjoy the thrill of the plot—the act of murder and bringing the killer to justice. But there also is commercial writing that has literary quality, in which the author takes pride. Sometimes it is a question whether to earn money for "undistinguished" writing or hold out for a market that may be smaller but will bring the respect the writer believes he has earned for superior craftsmanship and creativity.

In my essay I deal with the impact of Freud on the mystery. He exerted two main influences: the inclusion of the reasons *why* someone was driven to commit murder, in terms of his childhood fury and wish for revenge on cruel parents (revenge in a symbolic sense, unless the parents happen to be the actual targets of the murder); and the infiltration of sexual scenes into the once-puritanical mystery novel. Combining sex and murder, today's suspense story is difficult to top when artistically done.

All the writers in this book are hardworking authors or editors who over the years have made their living, or a good part of it, at the typewriter. As they plot the spilling of blood of mythical characters or the victims of real-life killers, they write with their own life's blood. And here, in these pages, they give us a glimpse of how they do it.

LUCY FREEMAN

ONE

On the Genre

1

Mayhem in the Mainstream: A Study in Bloodlines
Bruce Cassiday

- A man commits murder—several times—and another man pursues him, eventually bringing him to justice after laboriously tracking him down by intelligence, craft, and ingenuity.

This classic detective situation appears in a book recently marketed and reviewed as a mainstream novel to critical and public acclaim.

- A priest helps various couples untangle their marital problems with the aid of the Church. No murder occurs during the process.

A book detailing these interesting and complicated negotiations is currently marketed and reviewed as a detective novel to critical acclaim.

What is going on? How is a mystery buff supposed to track down novels of crime and murder when they hide under the guise of mainstream literature?

A more interesting question arises: Why is there a double standard in the publishing, marketing, and reviewing of certain novels which ordinarily would be called murder mysteries, novels of crime, or detective stories?

The first novel cited above, Ken Follett's *Eye of the Needle* (1978), belongs to the espionage school of literature, now accepted by many critics as a legitimate subtype of the detective novel. Originally published in Great Britain, the book was marketed in the United States as a mainstream novel to produce higher revenue.

The second novel, William X. Kienzle's *Mind over Murder* (1981), belongs to the Father Brown school of detection, a Catholic version of Harry Kemelman's Rabbi David Small. Although it contains no murder, it is marketed as a detective novel, the third in a series featuring Father Bob Koesler.

These examples are obviously exceptional—most mystery novels today are marketed as mysteries, and most mainstream novels are marketed as mainstream—but they point up an interesting fact in the evolution of the detective novel.

The fact is, a detective novel marketed as a mainstream novel today is apt to make more money than a detective novel marketed as such. The reason has to do with shifting public tastes and changing literary values. At one time, just after World War II, a novel marketed as a mystery had a better chance of making big money and achieving high sales figures than a mainstream novel; that is no longer true. The public is fickle; it tires of what it loves today and will hate it tomorrow.

The obvious question arises: What is the future of the detective novel? Is it finished?

The detective novel is far from finished. It has flexed its muscles and moved out into the mainstream and, as we shall see, has begun to exert a strong influence on the mainstream.

Let's digress and determine exactly what we mean by "detective novel" or a "novel of detection." By inference, a detective novel or novel of detection contains a crime, a criminal, clues, and a detective to solve the problem.

But *The Case of the Lucky Legs* (1933), an Erle Stanley Gardner detective novel that sold almost three and a half million copies, has no detective as protagonist; it features a defense lawyer, Perry Mason.

And what of *A Kiss Before Dying* (1953), Ira Levin's exceptional suspense novel, with its brilliant climax? The protagonist is the murderer; there is a victim but no detective.

Obviously, there should be a better word than "detective" to describe the detective novel. Murder mystery? Crime novel? Suspense novel? All have been suggested. "Mystery" is a good word but not unassailable; it hints at religious plays. "Crime" is a better word, for what murder mystery exists that has no crime? Unfortunately, the word "crime" has the connotation of a "true-crime" endemic in a Sunday supplement exposé. "Suspense"? Every good novel contains suspense, or it simply doesn't measure up to the standard rules of fiction.

Not only does the situation baffle readers, it confuses librarians as well, particularly those in charge of cataloguing books and putting them in their proper niches on the shelves. The woman in charge of my neighborhood public library claims she has one sure way of ascertaining whether a book is a mystery or a mainstream novel.

"If it's got a dead body in it, it's a mystery," she told me grandly.

But what, I countered, of *Hamlet*, of *Doctor Zhivago*, of *War and Peace*?

"Oh, we *know* what they are!"

Let's leave this intriguing problem hanging in the air for a moment and retreat in time to the beginnings of the murder mystery genre. Edgar Allan Poe, they say, began it all with his short story "The Murders in the Rue Morgue" (1841).

Yet murder, detectives, crime, and mystery had occurred in mainstream novels before Poe. The key point is that up to Poe not one novel was ever dedicated exclusively to a crime and its solution, as was Poe's short story.

However, in the same year Poe invented the detective story, Edward Bulwer Lytton published a novel in which he toyed with basic mystery elements. In *Night and Morning* the disinherited hero is involved with an underworld character in Paris during a raid on a counterfeiting operation. The counterfeiter is shot dead while following the hero during a daring escape from a building, using a rope suspended above an alley.

Lytton uses underworld cant. His "low" characters speak a beautiful fractured English.

"I *have* been lagged," one says. "Inquiries about your respectability would soon bring the bulkies about me; and you would not have poor Jerry sent back to the damned low place on t'other side of the herring-pond, would you?"

Translation: "Lagged" = imprisoned. "The bulkies" = the Bow Street runners, or police, big bruisers who "bulk out." "T'other side of the herring-pond" = Australia, the penal colony where criminals were sent, "herring-pond" being argot for ocean.

Lytton used other devices familiar to us today: a bureau dresser with a secret drawer containing proof of the hero's identity, a Parisian police detective infiltrated into a mob of criminals in headpiece and false eyepatch, the kidnaping of the heroine off a dark London street into a cab by one of the villains, blackmail by higher-ups.

In *Paul Clifford* (1830), a novel about a romantic rogue whose profession is highwayman, Lytton worked the story up to a sensational denouement in which a judge is forced to hang his only son—a good enough mystery plot even for today's audience. Note that the book predates Poe by eleven years.

In *Eugene Aram* (1832), Lytton went himself one better and novelized a true happening in which a murderer eluded the law for years before being brought to trial in a much-reported case; the protagonist went fiction one better by committing suicide in his cell on the eve of his hanging.

Bulwer Lytton was known as novelist who wrote mainstream novels.

Charles Dickens used detectives in his novels, too, yet none of his books except *The Mystery of Edwin Drood* (1870), which he did not live to finish, could be classified as a true detective novel.

Bleak House (1852) has a murder, a detective, a group of suspects, and an eventually unmasked murderer. Bucket—"Inspector Bucket of the Detective" as he calls himself—displays a surprising amount of the familiar hard-bitten rapacity of a twentieth-century detective when he tells the man he is arresting, "If that hundred guineas is to be made, it may as well be made by me as any other man." Interestingly enough, he nabs the wrong man; but eventually he turns up the murderess of Tulkinghorn. Apparently, he knew who she was all along.

Bucket is not above conning the suspect by letting her believe she has totally bamboozled him; he then sets his wife on her while she gets rid of the murder weapon—a Dickensian version of a later era's "smoking pistol"—by throwing it into a pond. The narrative even contains a coach chase (a search, actually) in which Bucket reasons his way to the quarry through a blinding snowstorm. Very traditional mystery stuff, yet Dickens wrote mainstream novels, sprawling, chaotic, and fun to read. It is interesting to note that Bucket predates the "first detective-novel detective" by sixteen years.

That man was, of course, Sergeant Cuff. The truth is that even William Wilkie Collins did not write a novel exclusively of detection in *The Moonstone* (1868). There are long passages that have nothing to do with the solution of the crime, just as in *Bleak House*. Yet he did introduce Sergeant Cuff in that book, the first police detective in what many call a novel of detection.

However, Collins had already anticipated twentieth-century crime fiction several years earlier in *Armadale* (1866), when he used an "inquiry agent"—what we now call a private detective—to track down a person in hiding.

The spirit of *Armadale* parallels later murder mysteries as much as the spirit of *The Moonstone*, with the use of four particularly modern conventions of the mystery:

• One character, following another, leaps into a hansom cab parked second in a cab rank in London and instructs the driver in ringing tones, in effect, to "follow that cab!"

"Double your fare, whatever it is," are his words to the driver, "if you keep the cab before you in view, and follow it wherever it goes."

• There are several instances in which inquiry agents are hired by characters in the novel.

"I went to the Private Inquiry Office in Shadyside Place," one character reports, later calling the detective hired an "inspector" and still later a "Confidential Agent." Where else but Shadyside Place would such an operative be found?

• To elude another inquiry agent, the female protagonist enters a ladies' shop, exits by a rear door, and escapes down a back alley.

"In a moment I was out in the mews—in another, I was in the next street—in a third, I hailed a passing omnibus, and was a free woman again," she relates.

• The same protagonist dresses a maidservant in her clothes and has her drive through the park and walk back to the house, showing her face in public. The maid then stands at the window of the apartment, looking out with her face in plain view of the agent in surveillance across the street. Thus the maid's face instead of the protagonist's is established in the eye of the detective.

Yet *Armadale* was a mainstream novel, 1866 version.

So much attention has been focused on Collins because of the success of *The Moonstone* and *The Woman in White* that many of his lesser books—less known even than *Armadale*—are ignored. But, like *Armadale*, many contain foreshadowings of modern mystery story elements.

- In *Man and Wife* (1870), a man plots to murder his wife through the help of a servant who he knows has murdered her own husband. The plot fails when the wife turns on the would-be murderer and destroys him instead.

- In *Law and the Lady* (1875), a wife learns that her husband has been tried for poisoning his first wife. The court handed down an equivocal verdict of "not proven"—a provision of Scotch law—letting him go free but not acquitting him. She sets out to prove his innocence even though he leaves her when he discovers that she knows about his shady past. Her clue-by-clue search accounts for most of the story.

- In *Blind Love* (1890), a man becomes involved in a scheme to substitute a dying consumptive for himself in order to collect his own life insurance through his wife.

Sound familiar? Good mystery elements all, yet all three were mainstream novels.

Four years before the publication of *Blind Love*, another mainstream writer of the time, Robert Louis Stevenson, single-handedly invented the psychological thriller when he wrote and published *Dr. Jekyll and Mr. Hyde* (1886). The novel was a sensation. But make note of the date. It was just one year later, in 1887, that another mainstream novelist was having trouble establishing himself as a serious historical novelist. In desperation, he produced a magazine potboiler titled *A Study in Scarlet*, about a detective who took on mystery cases the police found too difficult to solve.

His name was Arthur Conan Doyle.

Oddly enough, Doyle looked down his nose at mystery stories. He prided himself on writing "literature," such as *The White Company* (1891). He thought so little of the mystery short story that he did not consider it art at all but a kind of game.

Getting back to Stevenson, the creator of the most interesting split personality in literature had dabbled in mystery thrillers for some years.

His *New Arabian Nights* (1882) included stories of the Suicide Club and other "diversions."

Stevenson loved financial chicanery, high adventure, and pursuits bordering on the criminal. *The Wrecker* (1892) is a novel of skulduggery, narcotics smuggling, extortion, blackmail, and mass murder. One scene in particular has an extremely modern ring to it.

The hero identifies a criminal by deliberately listening to an adversary ask an operator for a telephone number; he then looks up the number in the San Francisco directory to find out the address and the adversary's identity. By the time he gets there, his quarry is gone.

A master of the genre?

Stevenson loathed "police" and "mystery" novels. On board a schooner, the hero of *The Wrecker* visits the ship's library, where he finds many books, including "a good many cheap detective books." But he can't really ignore detection. A few pages later, his hero writes: "I scanned his features with the eye of a detective." And later: "Who was to guess that one was a blackmailer, trembling to approach the scene of action—the other a helpless, amateur detective, waiting on events."

At one chapter ending he even sets up the puzzle: "Here at last," the narrator writes, "was the end of my discoveries; I learned no more, till I learned all; and my reader has the evidence complete. Is he more astute than I was? or, like me, does he give it up?"

He even takes a crack at a popular stage detective in Tom Taylor's *The Ticket-of-Leave Man*, when his narrator writes about his companion's "innocent reverence for the character of Hawkshaw," putting down a famed dramatic detective of the era.

Stevenson was writing mystery without admitting it; he was even writing mystery criticism without admitting it. But in the epilogue of *The Wrecker* he is writing from the heart when he explains how "attracted and repelled" he is "by that very modern form of the police novel or mystery story." Particularly, he goes on, he is "repelled by that appearance of insincerity and shallowness of tone, which seems its inevitable drawback." The reader's mind, he thinks, "always bent to pick up clews," is entrapped in an "airless, elaborate mechanism." Although the book might remain "enthralling," it is, of necessity, "insignificant, like a game of chess, not a work of human art."

He was obviously pointing the finger at A. Conan Doyle, the man who really caused the detective novel to become established as a literary genre.

Conan Doyle's creation, Sherlock Holmes, is a modernized version of Poe's Dupin, the amateur problem solver depending strictly on his intellect; he instantly became the prototype of the twentieth-century detective hero. The operative word here is "amateur." Dickens's Bucket, Collins's Cuff, and even Taylor's Hawkshaw were members of the police force. Collins experimented with the professional, non-police force detective in *Armadale*, but the inquiry agent was never a main character in any sense.

Poe got it right in the beginning by making Dupin an "amateur" detective, and Doyle followed his lead. By pinning that mantle on the amateur, you could get at the real police. Through the nineteenth century and well into the twentieth, the readers of novels—the emerging middle and upper classes—were antipathetic to the police.

The common people didn't like the police because they were the "other guys." The middle class suspected them of chicanery and feared them. The upper class simply reviled them. There was very good reason for the writers, who knew their markets, not to eulogize the bad guys.

Dickens handled Bucket with kid gloves, giving him a scene or two but making him more a caricature than a person. Collins made Cuff a policeman working away from his usual jurisdiction and thus a foil to the locals.

From the beginning, the official police were the incompetents, the bunglers, the dupes. Doyle went Poe one better, setting up Holmes in the profession of detective rather than making him simply a "gifted amateur."

With Doyle, the promise of Poe was realized. The detective story and detective novel became set in format and tone. Within two decades, on both sides of the Atlantic, a new genre was growing by leaps and bounds. It was the Golden Age of detective fiction, when book publishers, critics, and librarians separated detective novels from mainstream novels and awarded them a special place on the shelves.

Well they might. With these novels of detection selling in high numbers, with circulating libraries enjoying wide usage, with housewives and white-collar clerks reading mystery stories for fun, the publishers knew that they had a good thing going.

In London, Agatha Christie was starting out her most auspicious career; she and Dorothy L. Sayers were producing novel after novel featuring detectives. In New York, Willard Huntington Wright, using the pseudonym S. S. Van Dine, was producing similar "detective" novels. Christie's Hercule Poirot, Sayers's Lord Peter Wimsey, and Van Dine's Philo Vance were the epitomes of the Golden Age of detective heroes.

There were many others, but it is not in the province of this essay to go into the details. It is enough to point out that at the turn of the century the detective novel, modeled on Doyle's inspiration, became a genre distinct from the mainstream novel.

In its bloodstream, however, were the seeds of destruction and thereby the eventual dissolution of the genre. Looking back, the seeds were always there. Let's observe the amateur detective, the gifted intellect, the problem-solving genius as he really was.

Lord Peter Wimsey

"I think," said his lordship mournfully, "I had better stop being the perfect English aristocrat and become the great detective after all. Fate seems to be turning my one-day romance into a roaring farce. If that is the dossier, let me have it. We'll see," he added with a faint chuckle, "what kind of a detective you make when you're left to yourself."

Philo Vance

"Now for a brief *causerie* with the sad and gentlemanly Mr. Pardee. I don't know what he can tell us, but I have a yearnin' to commune with him." . . . "That elephant doesn't belong there," he remarked casually, pointing to a tiny figure in the collection. "It's a *bunjinga*—decadent, don't y' know. Clever, but not authentic. Probably a copy of a Manchu piece." He stifled a yawn and turned toward Markham. "I say, old man, there's nothing more we can do. Suppose we toddle."

Hercule Poirot

"Not so. *Voyons*! One fact leads to another—so we continue. Does the next fact fit in with that? *A merveille*! Good! We can proceed. This next little fact—no! Ah, that is curious! There is something missing—a link in the chain that is not there. We examine. We search. And that little curious fact, that possibly paltry little detail that will not tarry, we put it here! . . . It is significant! It is tremendous!"

Unbelievable today. Wimsey comes across the years as a conceited prig, Vance as a posturing fop, Poirot as too cute for words.

It was the Detection Club, founded in 1928 by G. K. Chesterton, the father of Father Brown, that was somehow the beginning of the end of the fictional detective in the mold of Wimsey, Vance, and Poirot. The point of the writers' organization—to which you were invited, not let in—was to establish rules and regulations for the proper creation of mystery stories.

At the initiation ceremonies each writer had to swear "never to conceal a vital clue from the reader." Other rules and regulations were formulated as well, particularly in regard to the downplaying of passion and the diminishing of character elements that might tend to overshadow the reader's enjoyment of the puzzle and its solution.

Favored with hindsight, we see that when a group of creative artists sits down to draw up rules and regulations for the creation of their artifacts—in this case, detective novels—the end is in sight. Rules and regulations become numbers in a formula; feed the numbers into a computer and turn out any "puzzle" novel you choose.

What did happen to the detective novel of the time was that it turned into a puzzle rather than a novel, featuring the steps leading up to the murder and the steps leading up to the solution of the murder without paying attention to character, background, or even the lifestyles of the various people. I am exaggerating for effect, but in the inferior productions of the era, the novel of manners almost disappears to become an exercise in puzzle breaking.

Soon it became evident that anyone could put together a puzzle; the reader became a kind of crossword puzzle addict. While the puzzles reached heights of ingenuity that had never before been scaled, the narratives became dreary and unreadable. The detective novel slowly but surely atrophied, although its degeneration and debasement were not immediately evident in the productions of its more competent and inspired practitioners.

Stevenson had been right when he voiced his suspicions that a mystery story might resemble "a game of chess, not a work of human art."

However, the tide was slow to recede. During the Golden Age of the detective novel, the word "detective" was used freely in bookstores, in libraries, and in book reviews. Most newspapers added special columns to review the current publications in this popular type of novel. Circulating libraries built special shelves for mysteries; so did public libraries. Book publishers issued detective books regularly, so many a month, so many a year. The detective novel became a category novel like the romance, the Western, or the science-fiction novel.

The detective novel, which had started out as an exercise of man's ingenuity against the evil in other men but which now became a puzzle for the reader to try to solve, did not intrigue all readers—or writers, either.

One reviewer handling Van Dine's *Benson Murder Case* (1926) ridiculed its "preposterous" solution, pointing out that it defied elementary ballistics and a knowledge of ordinary police procedure: "The authorities, no matter how stupid the author chose to make them, would have cleared up the mystery promptly if they had been allowed to follow the most rudimentary police routine. But then what would there have been for the gifted Vance to do?"

The reviewer's name was Dashiell Hammett, an American writer and ex-Pinkerton detective who knew what he was talking about. In his reviews he snorted at Philo Vance's posturings, and in his writing he created an entirely different kind of crime novel, one without amateur detectives in the Wimsey and Vance tradition.

Hammett used private investigators in a direct line of descent from the inquiry agents of Collins. He was not alone. Raymond Chandler, too, decried the artificiality of the puzzle motif and wrote about flesh-and-blood people.

Inspired by the American defection from the country-manor school of mystery, new writers turned the detective novel into a more realistic form. The Great Depression had changed life everywhere; war clouds were forming over Europe. Reality was in; fantasy was out. The private detective became cynical, sarcastic, and real.

In these books, people died in agony; no one had ever died gruesomely in the Golden Age of detective novels, or if one did die, one did not bleed all over the rug. The Hammett school took what was left of the novel of manners, which had always been an integral part of the detective novel from the first, and wedded it to the novel of realism to make the novel of detection an entirely different thing.

Oddly enough, for many years these two diametrically opposed types of literature coexisted happily in the book stalls, both labeled as detective novels. But the split was evident to anyone who read them.

The lovers of manor houses preferred the puzzle plots; the lovers of action and menace preferred the realistic crime novel.

Simultaneously with the split in the mystery novel, there was a revolution in the book publishing industry: the invention of the paperback book in 1939. This meant that the public could be entertained by cheap reading matter. A two- or three-dollar book could be purchased for twenty-five cents. After the initial launching of this new format, it was obvious that a whole new reading market was out there. And what sold the most?

After the Bible and other standards, the public seemed to want detective novels: Erle Stanley Gardner, Christie, Ellery Queen (modeled at first on the puzzle novel but then on a more realistic type of novel of detection), Rex Stout (with his own Holmes and Watson cleverly combining Wolfe/Holmes as the leads and Goodwin/Watson as the foils), and later, Ross Macdonald and John D. MacDonald.

World War II had an even more permanent impact on the detective novel than the Great Depression. Hammett and Chandler had kept the detective and thrown out the fripperies of the old-manse murder and the had-I-but-known school. But after the war was over, new writers emerged who threw out even the detective and substituted blood and violence.

After all, millions of men both in England and the United States had lived for years in mud and filth, next to blood and death, hoping to survive. They were not interested in the unrealities of country homes and terrified maidens. They wanted action and explicit sex.

Mickey Spillane arrived on the publishing scene and threw out the detective and the puzzle, replacing them with high emotion, action, sadism, sex, and violence.

Somewhere along the line he obviously hit the right chord in the sense of appealing to the mass audience and selling books. Two of his novels—*I, the Jury* (1962) and *The Big Kill* (1952)—both bloody lessons in vengeance and sadism, sold over five million apiece in hardback and paperback. Five more titles sold over four million copies each. That was where the action was—in sex and slaughter.

Men and women who had never read a book before read Spillane. He became a cult figure almost from the beginning. Up from the comic books, he took over the entire publishing industry. Anything he wrote sold in the multimillions. Everywhere he produced imitators; like the puzzle writers before him, authors discovered that they could write this stuff with ease.

Nobody really produced anything like Spillane's prototypes, however. It wasn't that he was good; it was simply that he was an original. Imitators found to their sorrow that they didn't really have what Spillane had, particularly that stranglehold on the public's imagination.

But there were more forces ready to assault the detective novel category than just Spillane. Millions of male readers learned about action and adventure while serving in the armed services during World War II. They became dissatisfied with writing that exhibited any kind of fakery. *Tarzan of the Apes* (1914) with its never-never African jungle could never have survived in the 1940s and 1950s. Those men had seen it all; they wanted realism in their writing. They wanted action, a kind of remembrance of things past, when they had been at the center of the fire.

The detective novel vied for popularity with the old novel of adventure, in the tradition of H. Rider Haggard's *She* (1887) and *King Solomon's Mines* (1885) and Robert Louis Stevenson's *The Wrecker* (1892), with the World War II soldier substituted for the dilettante British world traveler of the turn of the century.

But the writers of adventure novels knew the power of the mystery mystique; they knew what their fans demanded of them. They acquired, transformed, and used as many plot and character elements of the detective novel as they could assimilate. What they created in a very short time resembled the novel of intrigue that had been developed at the turn of the century. In the postwar version, the adventure novel combined suspense, mystery, action, and espionage. Quite frequently, the protagonist was a secret agent—in the Secret Service in British novels, the OSS in American novels (later to become the CIA).

Adventure-suspense novels by Alistair MacLean, Hammond Innes, Desmond Bagley, and Andrew Garve were so close to mystery novels that many readers assumed they were reading mysteries. Later, Ian Fleming invented James Bond, the prototype of the destroyer with a mandate to kill and to make love to the beautiful girls.

This subgenre of the suspense novel traced its heritage back to Philip Raney in Lord Buchan's *Thirty-Nine Steps* (1915) and *Greenmantle*

(1916) and perhaps to Eric Ambler's early espionage novels, but there the resemblance ended. Instead of realistic chases and predicaments to contend with, Bond simply annihilated all his enemies with fascinating technological gimmicks too good to be true. Most of the time Fleming wrote with tongue in cheek; he was tired of real espionage and wanted to dream of what it could have been like without all the bloodshed.

The adventure-suspense novelists concentrated on the British out-doorsman covering the globe in the style of Rudyard Kipling, Stevenson, and Haggard. Some purists, incidentally, refuse to accept the espionage novel that emerged as part of the mystery genre; they posit the theory that the protagonist is not a detective at all but a spy.

However, there is a great deal of Poe's ratiocination involved in intelligence work; for example, cryptography is one of the spy's main means of survival. And there is action as well, along with the detectival crafts of surveillance, deduction, and the piecing together of evidence.

I consider the secret agent a man of detective talents working for a country rather than for a police force or a paying individual client. Most publishers immediately accepted the spy story as a part of the mystery genre. It was to become one of the most important of the subgenres in a few years.

There was another even more crucial defection from the detective format of the Golden Era. As I have mentioned, Dickens and Collins had toyed with the idea of a policeman as detective protagonist almost a hundred years earlier, but the reading public wasn't there. Now it quite evidently was there.

Detective novels began appearing with policemen as protagonists and even heroes, in books by Larry Treat, Hillary Waugh, Ed McBain (Evan Hunter), and eventually J. J. Marric (John Creasey) and Joseph Wambaugh. The study of the police detective at work and play became a new subgenre, the "police procedural."

The puzzle mystery did not actually die; the whodunit continued in an uninterrupted line from the Golden Age, as witness Ellery Queen, Agatha Christie, Rex Stout, and Erle Stanley Gardner. So did the hard-boiled private eye novel, in many different manifestations but most importantly in the novels of Ross Macdonald and John D. MacDonald.

But many writers felt confined by the format and added socio-logical and political overtones in compliance with the changing tastes

of the public. One spin-off of the detective novel eventually branched
out into a most viable subgenre: the geopolitical thriller of the 1960s
and 1970s.

The doomsday theme, with the protagonist saving the world on
the last page from nerve gas, atom bombs, or mystery viruses, produced
thrillers of the kind written by Tom Ardies and John Lange (Michael
Crichton). Closely allied to the geopolitical mystery was the sociopol-
itical mystery, in which the protagonist tried to survive amid social
unrest, technological disaster, or political confrontation in novels by
Jack Higgins and Peter Driscoll.

Psychologists interested in reasons more than in the overt violence
that sprang from the reasons developed another subgenre, the psychological mystery. In this type of novel, the psychological implications
of murder and violence, the psychological interplay between hunter
and hunted, and the various nuances of psychological illnesses received
the full attention of writers such as Margaret Millar, Dorothy Salisbury
Davis, and later, Lucy Freeman.

Other writers, going back to Lytton and the Victorian novelists,
turned the hero inside out and wrote about the criminal, producing the
"caper" novel that stressed the crime and its perpetrators and their
problems rather than the detective in pursuit of them, in the style of
W. R. Burnett's *Asphalt Jungle* (1949) and Eric Ambler's *The Light of
Day*.

More splits appeared in the fragmenting genre as the 1960s rolled
on into the 1970s. The Gothic was reinvigorated in the hands of Victoria Holt, Mary Stewart, and Phyllis Whitney. Many students of the
detective novel refused to recognize the Gothic in its twentieth-century
manifestation as part of the genre, but it was.

The old-fashioned novel of pursuit—the chase—soon became a
male counterpart to the Gothic, with the male in distress rather than
the damsel in distress. Eric Ambler, Geoffrey Household, and their
fellow practitioners transformed Victor Hugo's Javert–Valjean combination into many variations rich and strange, with police, detectives,
spies, and ordinary men in the street acting as hunter and hunted.

Some thoughtful writers went Mickey Spillane one step further
and created the vigilante mystery, in which the hero became his own
judge, jury, and executioner, pointing the finger of criticism at the

ineffectiveness of the court system. Such writers included Joe Gores, Brian Garfield, and Bill Pronzini.

Writers interested in the world of technology developed the "mechanistic mystery," stressing the mechanics of business and/or politics: the money game, the computer game, the genes game, the terrorist game, the power game, and so on. These writers included Paul E. Erdman, Michael Crichton, and others.

The mystery novel even got ribbed by stand-up comics, with the "camp" mystery popular for a short period. Donald E. Westlake led the pack, and others, including Robert L. Fish, participated. Then history buffs got into the act and combined history and mystery to produce the period-piece mystery, with practitioners such as John Dickson Carr, Robert van Gulick, and Peter Lovesy.

In short, nothing was sacred any more; the tight strictures that had bound the Golden Age detective novel together to make it into a genre of perfection were broken and would never be tied together again.

Because there were so many different facets of the mystery novel, the public became confused. In retrospect, what happened seems obvious, although at the time it was not quite so clear. A World War II veteran would pick up a book in the mystery section of either a paperback store or a library, take it home, and find out he was reading a woman's Gothic or a puzzle novel which he didn't want to read. A Gothic fan would pick up a paperback and find to her horror that it was a Spillane-type blood-and-guts thriller. Or a political liberal would pick up a police procedural and go through the roof at being asked to empathize with a flatfoot on the bricks.

In addition, there was a great deal of confusion in publishing circles. Reviewers who used to cover only mysteries had no idea what they were getting into any more. Even writers of detective stories became disenchanted with the kind of product they were involved in. The detective novel had become something that wasn't really what it should have been. When any product becomes suspect, the men in charge turn against it, trying to turn it out of the market before it spoils the rest of the produce.

Listen to what the writers themselves had to say about the detective novel in that period:

Echoing the sentiments of Stevenson and Doyle, Raymond Chandler wrote in the 1950s, "To accept a mediocre form and make something like literature out of it is in itself rather an accomplishment." In other words, even he didn't think much of the medium in which he was working.

And critic Edmund Wilson: "With so many fine books to be read . . . there is no need to bore ourselves with this rubbish"—meaning the detective novel.

So what do you do if you love the craft you're an expert at but know that it's getting a bad shake from the public and the critics? You do exactly what Robert Louis Stevenson had done and what Daphne du Maurier distinguished herself by doing in the 1930s: You write a mystery and pretend that it isn't.

By combining the Gothic spirit with a murder plot, Du Maurier had written one of the most celebrated mystery novels of the era in *Rebecca*, a book that was marketed as a mainstream novel with no mention of its mystery elements. Obviously, it was a superior piece of detective novel writing, yet its publishers did not want it to be considered a "detective" story.

Likewise Meyer Levin, who published *Compulsion* in 1956. It was a carefully researched novelization of the Loeb and Leopold murder trial, but the book was marketed as a mainstream work rather than a nonfiction murder mystery. When a Michigan judge turned his hand to fiction two years later, writing a novel based on a famous trial with which he was familiar, he published *Anatomy of a Murder* under the pseudonym of Robert Traver as a mainstream novel, although it too was a murder mystery in the old tradition.

The classic case of the mainstream novel that was really a detective novel was *The Spy Who Came in from the Cold*, published in 1964. Both John Le Carré and his publisher didn't want the novel to become lost in the detective novel category so that it could be stigmatized as a James Bond imitation. They had reason to worry. The author had already written two novels: a spy novel, *Call for the Dead*, marketed as such in 1961, and a detective novel, *A Murder of Quality*, marketed as such in 1962. Neither had done well.

For Le Carré, the mainstream marketing technique developed to promote *Spy* provided spectacular results in hot sales figures and cold hard cash. The book became a runaway bestseller and was the number one fiction hit of the year, racking up 230,000 sales in hardcover, a very impressive figure. It was, in one of the new terms being bandied about in the publishing world, a "blockbuster."

It was becoming obvious to publishers that these "big books" were making out, no matter what kind of material they contained. Truman Capote had enjoyed great prestige in American letters but had sold relatively small numbers of books, when in 1966 he came out with a fictionalized fact-crime story "ripped from the headlines of the day," as a blurb-writer might put it.

In Cold Blood was marketed in a slightly different fashion, however. Fact crime was not mentioned. The book was called a "nonfiction novel," a new departure, and it sailed into print in the mainstream rather than be tarred and besmirched by fact-crime associations.

Shades of Edward Bulwer Lytton, who novelized the story of Eugene Aram but wasn't above admitting he had fictionalized a man's life in order to bring it between book covers. Lytton did not, however, categorize his book as a nonfiction novel. He would have thought the term an unacceptable oxymoron.

"I have exercised the common and fair license of writers of fiction," he wrote. "It is chiefly the more homely parts of the real story that have been altered; and for what I have added, and what omitted, I have the sanction of all established authorities, who have taken greater liberties with characters yet more recent, and far more protected by historical recollections."

The cases Capote and Lytton celebrated in their books, separated by two hundred years, were both characterized by the death of a murderer in his prison environment, an eerie similarity for such celebrated and highly publicized cases.

By 1967 it was obvious that strange things were happening in the publishing world. The mystery genre had seemingly broken out of its mold to become a kind of mainstream literary freak. A story of the eerie and supernatural, *Rosemary's Baby*, written by Ira Levin, got onto the bestseller list that year, with almost a hundred thousand copies sold in hardcover. So did *The Gabriel Hounds*, a Gothic by Mary Stewart, with 76,000 copies. A suspense novel with political overtones and murder called *Topaz*, by Leon Uris, was one of the ten best with over a hundred thousand sales.

These books, which ordinarily might have been published as mystery novels, were marketed as mainstream novels in an attempt to cash in on the big money generated by Le Carré's breakthrough.

But it was not until 1971 that the "blockbuster complex" became an established fact. Frederick Forsyth had written *The Day of the Jackal*, a fictionalized chase story of the imagined assassination of Charles de Gaulle. Although specifically an espionage thriller, it was sold in the mainstream—and it sold very well. Forsyth's second novel, *The Odessa File* (1972), did well also, as did his fourth, *The Devil's Alternative* (1980). Forsyth was paid $10,000 for *Jackal*, $500,000 for *Odessa*, and almost $2 million for *Alternative*.

By that time, it was rare for a year to go by without at least one good mystery novel in the top ten bestsellers. *The Exorcist*, by William Blatty, appeared in 1971, and sold over one hundred fifty thousand; *The Matlock Papers*, by Robert Ludlum, sold almost a hundred thousand in the same year. Paul E. Erdman's *The Billion Dollar Sure Thing* sold almost as many copies.

In 1974 Sherlock Holmes reappeared in Nicholas Dreyer's *The Seven Percent Solution*, running ninth for the year with sales of about a hundred thousand. In 1978 Sidney Sheldon appeared with *Bloodline*, a thriller with some crime elements. The same year, *Eye of the Needle* appeared, selling over one hundred thousand for Ken Follett. And in 1979 Stephen King came in number six with *The Dead Zone*, reaching almost two hundred thousand copies. But 1979 was a banner year for the mystery novel. Robert Ludlum's *The Matarese Circle* became number one for the year, the first time since 1964, when John Le Carré's *Spy* was number one.

To backtrack a moment, Blatty's novel, although supernatural, definitely fulfilled the requirements of the mystery novel. Modeled in the same tradition as an earlier blockbuster, *Rosemary's Baby*, it represented a neat blending of the modern mystery novel with the nineteenth-century supernatural novel—*Dracula* and *Frankenstein*—and earlier versions such as *The Castle of Otranto* and *The Monk*.

By the 1970s, most bookstores and some libraries were devoting subsections of the mystery to "horror" and "fantasy," largely as a result of the Levin and Blatty novels. To skip ahead to 1979, the novels of Stephen King were beginning to catch on after a slow start with *Carrie*

(1974) and *The Shining* (1977). By now the suspense-horror novel was a natural subgenre of the detective novel.

Ludlum's offering, *The Matlock Papers*, represented one of the most interesting developments in the "blockbuster mystery," if we can call it that. In the days of Sayers and Chesterton, such a sprawling, big novel as Ludlum's might never have been considered a mystery novel. Nor, actually, is it. But it contains enough suspense elements and criminal endeavors to be perfectly compatible with the detective label. Like Stevenson, Ludlum eschewed the detective label and sought the adventure label.

Erdman's novel of financial chicanery was a typical mechanistic novel of a particular phase of high finance. Along with its suspense and mystery elements, it provided a peek into the fascinating world of money: a kind of comedy of manners of the gold room.

Sidney Sheldon is not considered by many literate and knowledgeable mystery readers as a mystery writer, but *Bloodline* has elements of suspense, attempted murder, and mystery that bring it into the genre.

Follett's first work, *Eye of the Needle*, was an espionage novel, a follow-up on the kind of thing Le Carré was doing in his Smiley novels. Follett produced a chase novel, an updated *Les Miserables* placed in World War II.

Meanwhile, strange things were happening to the mystery genre itself during the period of the blockbuster and the big novel. Let's go back to the end of the 1960s. The detective novel was selling well, with about five hundred titles—that is, individual novels—published each year. In 1970, the figure rose to about six hundred; and in 1971, to seven hundred. That's a lot of mystery books.

But in 1972, the figure dropped to 502; in 1973, to 372, where it lingered for a few years in the vicinity, only to plummet in 1976 to 204. By 1978, the figure was 128, and in 1979, *Publishers Weekly* stopped listing mysteries as category books.

By comparing the years, you can see that as the figures for the mystery per se declined, the figures for the blockbuster mystery—aka mainstream novel—were rising.

Obviously, according to the category figures, the mystery, detective, suspense, Gothic, or crime novel was dead. But when was the wake held? Who attended? Who gave the eulogy? Why was it not made known to the public or to the writers, who should be the first to know? The truth of the matter is that the mystery was not dead at all but had changed into something else. It had shucked its label and was unrecognizable as a genre any more. Where had it gone? To the very top of the best seller list—as it should have gone.

In reviewing the bestselling novels of the 1970s, *Publishers Weekly* reported that the "suspense genre was clearly the favorite category for reading entertainment."

And yet, by that time, in a totally contradictory fashion, the magazine was no longer recognizing mystery/suspense/detective as a category.

A look at the bestsellers for the year 1980 explains why *Publishers Weekly* was so high on suspense:

#2.   *The Bourne Identity*. Robert Ludlum. 325,000 copies in hardcover
#3.   *Rage of Angels*. Sidney Sheldon
#5.   *Firestarter*. Stephen King. 285,000 copies in hardcover
#6.   *The Key to Rebecca*. Ken Follett
#8.   *The Devil's Alternative*. Frederick Forsyth. 129,000 copies in hardcover
#15. *The Tenth Commandment*. Lawrence Sanders. 129,000 copies in hardcover

Suspense was in, in 1980. Mystery was in. So was bulk.

During the Golden Era, the detective novel ran anywhere from 55,000 to 75,000 words in length. Writers and editors tried to keep the story confined to that limit because it made marketing easier and it made paperback reprint publication more systematic and therefore profitable.

The blockbuster syndrome brought in length and weight. Le Carré. Forsyth. Sheldon. Follett. King.

A brief word about construction and style. During the Golden Age of detective fiction, each mystery novel was carefully plotted, with chapter breaks appearing at exactly the right point in the rising action, with little bits of red herring strewn about to throw the reader off the scent.

The scenes themselves were carefully structured, following the style of dramatic dialogue and action familiar to stagegoers. The ripostes of dialogue made for good dramatic give-and-take, leading up to a breaking off at a high point of suspense.

You could count the number of scenes in a mystery novel and find that there were just about as many as in another work by the same author, provided that the length was about the same.

Descriptive material was kept to a minimum, but the need to paint a picture always remained. The scenes were done in leisurely fashion, but when finished, they were adroitly tied off to lead into further action.

There was a modicum of characterization; when it was done, it was done stylishly and with conviction. Hair coloring, face, eyes, lips, and figure were described in order to give the reader a chance to "see" the character.

In certain instances, such as the mystery novels of Erle Stanley Gardner, it was the author's intention never to describe Perry Mason or Della Street. But other characters sometimes were described.

Hammett and Chandler and the school of the hard-boiled op handled style in almost the same manner. The pace was faster, but only moderately so.

At about the time the blockbusters came in, big changes were occurring in the publishing business. Off in the wings, ever since the end of World War II, there waited a giant-killer; its name was television. It was waiting to take over the entire publishing business and wipe out all the print in the world in order to substitute pictures that moved.

Using motion picture technique, television speeded up its dramas, intercutting short scenes to sustain suspense, focusing on details that needed attention, and establishing complicated setting in the flash of a frame.

Dialogue. Drama. Action.

You sat in front of the set and saw a scene in ten seconds. On paper, you would read at least sixty seconds, or perhaps ninety seconds, to assimilate the same amount of information.

You perceived instantly from television. You didn't want a lot of stuff about the flowers and the trees. You *knew* you were in a field. You saw it. You didn't want long description or long internal soliloquies.

Action. Violence.

The writers of print material knew that they were competing with television—for their lives. They couldn't beat the electronic medium,

and so they joined it, after a fashion. They adapted the techniques of
film to print. They had to. Viewers were impatient with time. Action
had to crackle. Dialogue had to sparkle. The attention span of the
viewer was shrinking day by day.

The scene Dorothy Sayers spun out for perhaps five pages had
become three pages in the hands of the hard-boiled private eye writer.
In the hands of the blockbuster writer, doing mystery but calling it
mainstream, the scene finished in perhaps a half page.

Print manuscripts began to fragment:

A scene breaks. There's a space. The writer has no time to compose
a transition. The white space means that the film cuts.

Here's Robert Ludlum ending one sequence in which a man is
killed, to begin another in an entirely different setting and time:

The Monk lunged forward; there was nothing left but a final gesture, a
final defiance. The European fired.

SPACE

The door of the brownstone opened. From the shadows beneath the stair-
case the chauffeur smiled. The White House aide. . . .

It drives you to distraction sometimes, but by the time you realize
you are annoyed, you're well into the next scene and you pick up what
you've missed—or discover that you don't need to pick anything up
at all. Because there's nothing there any more, and there's more action
ahead.

Always action.

Quick cuts. Montages. Short buildups. Dialogue. Bang, bang. White
space. Paragraph: "The pockmarked beggar scratched the stubble of
his beard. . . ." And you're into another sequence.

Or take Stephen King, who breaks his chapters into segments,
each numbered.

"Get away," she hissed. "Take your monster and get away."

15.

OJ ran.
The Windsucker bounced up and down under his arm as he ran.

It almost becomes a parody of see Spot run, but it isn't quite. It's
telling a story in a way that is familiar to people weaned on television,
with its great visuals and tiny insights.

Using this technique, it is obvious that a writer can tell a story in a lot less space than in the old days. Sayers's five pages becomes a half page; the one hundred thousand words of a Sayers novel thus becomes a ten thousand-word novelette.

But there are tricks to the technique. In a trade-off for action, the blockbuster writer leans heavily on dialogue and lets the characters talk and talk between bouts of action.

Sometimes pages and pages of dialogue between two people follow a quick and brutal scene of action. The dialogue tends to be brusque.

"What was in the envelope?"

"I told you, I did not open it."

"But you know what was in it."

"Money, I presume."

"You *presume*?"

"Very well. Money. A great deal of money. If there was any discrepancy, it had nothing to do with me. Now *please*, I *beg* you. Get *out* of here!"

"One last question."

"*Anything*. Just leave!"

"What was the money for?"

Note that the two main ingredients of the blockbuster novel are action and dialogue—exactly the same two main ingredients that make up a film.

Even so, the fact that the blockbuster book, to be big, must have a lot of pages forces the writer to pack in more incident, plot, and characters than in a comparable detective novel of the Golden Era. To take up the slack, the author invents a lot more story than he might otherwise.

To make more story, the writer covers more ground. You're in Washington. The scene ends. You're at Orly Airport. Suddenly you cut, and you're in Nairobi. Then you're at the Taj Mahal. In front of the Beverly Hills police station. The Vieux Carré in New Orleans. The Astrodome. The Louvre.

Movement.

Action.

And because you cover more territory, you need more characters: medium-main characters, minor-main characters, minor characters, mini-minor characters, mini-mini-minor characters.

Frequently, in a novel with a great deal of mayhem in it, a character may be introduced in one scene for the specific reason that he or she can be blown to bits at the end of it!

More characters. More scenes. More countries. More girth. More weight. A higher cover price. More money in the writer's pocket.

If the typically tightly plotted detective novel of the Golden Age contained a handful of characters, concentrating on perhaps three or four at the most, the big novel of today contains a dozen to start with and adds more and more before coming to the end.

Examples: The size of the average bestselling blockbuster novel— *not* the mystery novel—may run from 178,000 words (*Firestarter*) to 244,000 (*Bourne*).

Reminiscent of Charles Dickens, Edward Bulwer Lytton, Wilkie Collins.

We are somehow right back where we started—in the mainstream, with huge casts of characters, big overblown books, and words, words, words.

Dickens's *Bleak House*: 383,000 words.

But I love them, as talky and bloated as they are, because they keep me turning the pages over and over.

Meanwhile, the somewhat fragmented but still vigorous detective novel, which is not masquerading as something it isn't but is still unpretentiously being exactly what it wants to be, continues to swim along slightly outside the mainstream, attracting new and exciting writers to its form in the persons of P. D. James, Ruth Rendell, Gregory Mcdonald, and many others.

It's only the public that is baffled by the labels. We know what we are. And so do our fans.

2

The Case for the Private Eye

Thomas Chastain

The introduction of the private eye into detective fiction is probably the most important contribution the United States has made to mystery literature.

According to most authoritative sources, the character of the private eye was born in the pages of *Black Mask* magazine, the best of the detective pulp magazines of the 1930s and 1940s.

The character was an inspired creation, ideally suited to serve the needs of American mystery writers seeking to avoid imitation of their British peers.

Tough, hard-boiled, here was a character born to speak the spare, blunt language of "Americanese," a distinctive new voice in writing (elsewhere, in other forms, other writers such as Ernest Hemingway also were experimenting in this direct, stripped-down prose style).

More than that, the private eye character was a loner—in the mold of the knight in armor and the cowboy in gun belt—who had the potential for achieving the proportions of a mythic figure.

But this is intellectualizing after the fact. At the time, the private eye might well have been confined to the pages of *Black Mask*, except that two writers, Dashiell Hammett and Raymond Chandler, took the character and made of him and of the private eye story something considerably more than a device for telling another entertaining tale. They created a whole new genre in mystery fiction.

Both men were contributing stories to *Black Mask* magazine at the time. As everyone knows by now, Hammett had been a real-life detective with the Pinkerton agency, and he used some of his own experiences as a basis for the first of his stories published in the magazine.

Then came *The Maltese Falcon*, which appeared as a serial in *Black Mask* and then in hardcover. The classic form of the private eye novel was set for all time.

Raymond Chandler, who has always been generous in his acknowledgment of the literary debt he owed Hammett, took the form and contributed his own epigrammatic style. From that day to this, no writer has been able to improve on the form or even to come close to equaling the work of these two writers, in my opinion. God knows that plenty of writers have tried down through all the years since then. Moving from pulp magazines to hardcover and softcover books came a proliferation of shamuses, gumshoes, and PIs.

A few of them were pretty good, some were only so-so, and a lot were plain awful. But the form proved amazingly durable. Now, after almost half a century, the private eye story is still going strong in books, in motion pictures and most of all, on television (after having proved itself a staple of radio). And all those writers and their books did their part in keeping the tradition alive.

From time to time the private eye character underwent certain physical changes in an attempt at originality on the part of his creators. Thus we have had one-armed private eyes, black private eyes, homosexual private eyes, and female private eyes. Yet none of them ever managed to alter the form cast by Hammett and Chandler (as Hammett and Chandler did when they first established the form of the private eye novel, as distinct from other mystery fiction).

There have, of course, been notable contributions to the genre, foremost among them Ross Macdonald's Lew Archer novels. In his long string of literately written private eye novels, Macdonald has remained close to Hammett and Chandler and yet has still managed to be his own man. If nothing else, he stands apart from all the others by attempting to recast the private eye story into the larger dimensions of the mainstream novel.

I do not include John D. MacDonald and his hero, Travis McGee, in this discussion of private eyes; to me a private eye must be exactly that: a character who clearly labels himself, and makes his living at being, a private investigator. Not a newspaperman, or an adventurer, or a gentleman—or whatever. Having said this, I hasten to add that it is my opinion that John D. MacDonald is the finest craftsman writing today, anywhere.

To get back to the basic sources of the genre, back to Hammett and Chandler again, I would like to suggest reasons why any writer or reader of private eye novels ought to get back to them again and often—especially to two of their books, Hammett's *The Maltese Falcon* and Chandler's *The Big Sleep*.

It's all there in those two books, everything the private eye novel is all about or ever will be. Story, character, style—all the elements that make the private eye novel a pleasure to read and, if an author is successful, a satisfaction to write.

I have a theory about writing which goes something like this: Writing can't be taught, but it can be learned, and the way you learn is by reading the work of other writers. In the mystery field, the two writers I learned most from were Hammett and Chandler, and the books were *The Maltese Falcon* and *The Big Sleep*.

Hammett, naturally, did it first. In *The Maltese Falcon*, Sam Spade's partner, Miles Archer, is killed early in the story. Then Spade becomes involved with the whole business of the priceless statuette, the Maltese falcon, and it is only after the statuette is disposed of that Spade solves the mystery of who killed his partner.

In *The Big Sleep*, Chandler's Philip Marlowe takes on a case of blackmail and discovers early on that a man is missing, is believed to have skipped out. Marlowe gets involved in a complicated puzzle of blackmail, and it is only after the blackmail case is resolved that he is able to solve the mystery of the missing man—that he was killed—and who killed him.

In other words, in both books the authors deliberately misdirect the eye (the private eye of the story and the eye of the reader) while working toward the solution of the mystery. Interestingly enough, in both books the mystery posed in the story was contained in the subplot while the main plot line was given over to what was essentially the misdirection of the eye.

When I wrote my suspense novel *Pandora's Box* (1974), I not only used this device which I had learned from Hammett and Chandler but had my characters explain that they were deliberately misdirecting the eye. *Pandora's Box* is a story about the robbery of the Metropolitan

Museum of Art in Manhattan, and the main plot line concerns how the thieves go to great lengths to set up a misdirection of the eye to hide how they pull off the robbery and where they conceal the five priceless paintings they've stolen.

Later on, when I wrote my own private eye novel, *Vital Statistics* (1977), I tried to use everything I had learned from Hammett and Chandler.

Again, I employed the device of misdirection of the eye. In *Vital Statistics* my private detective, J. T. Spanner, is involved in a case in which a dead girl's body is stolen while en route to the morgue and with another case in which an airline stewardess is missing. In Spanner's investigation of the two cases—are the dead girl and the missing stewardess the same person?—he discovers the existence of a plot employing a priceless jewel, the Sancy diamond. It is only after Spanner disposes of the puzzle of the diamond that he is able to solve the other mysteries.

In *Vital Statistics* I tried to pay my literary debt to Hammett and Chandler in a short sequence in which Spanner is talking to an old private eye who mentions that he once worked in California. Spanner asks him if he ever ran into a couple of private eyes out there named Spade and Marlowe, and the old guy says no. Then Spanner says: "Marlowe operated around L. A., and Spade worked in San Francisco. A couple of straight guys from all I've heard. They did a lot for the business."

A small bit, meant mostly for fun—which is another thing I learned about writing the private eye novel from Hammett and Chandler. They both believed that it should be fun to write and read, no matter how serious your intentions as a writer.

There are many instances of this in *The Maltese Falcon*, but I'll pick a couple of sentences from the book in which Caspar Gutman, the fat man, speaks. He says to Spade: "Now, sir, we'll talk if you like. And I'll tell you right out that I'm a man who likes talking to a man that likes to talk."

That's lovely writing, and it must have been fun to write.

Or take the opening sentence of *The Big Sleep*: "It was about eleven o'clock in the morning, mid October, with the sun not shining and a look of hard wet rain in the clearness of the foothills. . . ."

As nice a sentence as they come, particularly "with the sun not shining." It's much more fun to say "cloudy" that way.

Hammett and Chandler had style. Sentence by sentence, they used the language in a way that's fun to read.

As I mentioned earlier, private eye films have long been popular and have done much to keep the tradition alive. Once again Hammett and Chandler set the attitude, tone, and style for so many of the private eye films which have followed and are still being made.

Both books were well served in their film versions by having Humphrey Bogart portray first Sam Spade and then Philip Marlowe. Bogart himself was to go on in the years after to become something of a mythic figure in his own right; it's interesting that although the two private eyes are more dissimilar than similar in appearance, speech, and attitude between book covers, Bogart managed to become the quintessential Spade and Marlowe on film. Also, while it's true that Bogart left his imprint on the two characters, it also might be true that they left their imprint on the actor's persona as he went on in motion pictures.

If it is true, as I believe, that the motion picture versions of *The Maltese Falcon* and *The Big Sleep* have tended to reinforce the novels themselves, by repeated showings over television and in theaters, it also is true that both films were particularly faithful to their books. (*The Maltese Falcon* was additionally well served by having John Huston as its director. Huston did a remarkable job of keeping his camera completely objective in filming *The Maltese Falcon*, totally nonintrusive, as Hammett had done in writing the book, standing back from the story. *The Maltese Falcon*, told by Hammett in the third person, is totally different in that concept from *The Big Sleep*, which is told by Chandler in the first person.)

Finally, I want to say that to me one of the most stimulating aspects about reading, or writing in, a traditional form such as the private eye story is the awareness that each writer and each novel is creating a variation on a theme. That becomes a very real challenge, at least for a writer with enough imagination. And the best of these writers do something else; they suggest how the very limitations of the traditional form might be transcended.

Will there always be a case to be made for the private eye? Once, for fun, I speculated that since Sam Spade lost his partner Miles Archer, maybe he and Philip Marlowe might meet and go into partnership: "Spade and Marlowe." They'd still retain their separate offices, Spade in San Francisco, Marlowe in Los Angeles; that way, they could cover most of the state of California. Naturally, they would visit back and forth when the need arose. They'd probably get along well enough since basically they're pretty much the same underneath their shared surface cynicism; both knowledgeable, caring, concerned individuals. And they'd play off well against each other, Spade more hard-bitten and laconic, Marlowe coming on brash and wisecracking.

In this new relationship a man would show up one day in their San Francisco office, telling Spade that he had no knowledge of who he was, no knowledge of his past, and that he was troubled because somewhere dimly in his consciousness he believed he had witnessed a series of murders in San Francisco and Los Angeles. He would want to hire Spade and Marlowe to discover his true identity. Spade would call Marlowe to San Francisco. They would start running down unsolved murders in both cities while investigating all sources to establish the man's identity. It would begin to appear that there was a connection between a series of unsolved cases in both cities, and meanwhile they would be unable to turn up any ID on the man, nothing to prove he had ever existed. The man would then vanish as abruptly as he had appeared, leaving no trace.

And then . . .

3

The Human Rather Than Superhuman Sleuth

Hillary Waugh

The police procedural detective story is the second variation in the form of the art since the modern mystery took shape in what can be called the Golden Age, or classical period, of the genre, back in the 1920s.

Sherlock Holmes, of course, was the inspiration for all detective fiction that followed his arrival on the scene. While it is true that Conan Doyle patterned his creation along the lines of Poe's Auguste Dupin and followed Poe's technique of having the detective's feats recorded by a faithful friend, Holmes was so dominant a figure that Dupin's impact was ever after either overlooked or forgotten.

The modern mystery or detective story did not start with Holmes, however. An important ingredient was missing from the Holmes tales. In them, the reader is but a witness, standing at Watson's shoulder while the good doctor watches the great man unravel the threads of mystery and then proceeds to explain how he did it. The change that modernized the mystery came when the reader was elevated from the position of witness to that of participant. The moment the reader was engaged in competition with the detective in an effort to beat him to the solution, a radical change occurred. The element of fair play became an ingredient in the game. No longer could Sherlock feed poisoned pills to an aged dog while Watson wondered what he was up to. Fair play required that the reader be given an equal chance to deduce that they were poisoned. In short, the new rules of the game required that

33

all the clues available to the detective be made available to the reader. Once that change was made, the pattern of the present-day detective story was set.

The first response to this requirement produced the classical period of the mystery genre and brought to the fore such authors and detectives as Agatha Christie with her Hercule Poirot, Dorothy Sayers with Lord Peter Wimsey, Earl Derr Biggers with Charlie Chan, S. S. Van Dine with Philo Vance, Frederic Dannay and Manfred Lee with Ellery Queen, and Rex Stout with Nero Wolfe.

The aim of the game in this period was to fool the reader. While the author had to give the reader all the necessary clues to solve the case, nothing was said about how they were to be given. Authors secreted them among trivia, diluted them with red herrings, misinterpreted them through the detective, or slipped them into the story while distracting the reader through misdirection. All of this was aimed toward the goal of producing, as the villain at the end of the story, the "least suspected" character. Without question, no one could do this more successfully than Agatha Christie, and never more effectively than in *The Murder of Roger Ackroyd*.

The presentation of these puzzle stories usually followed the line of pitting a supergenius detective against a supergenius criminal who invented the most intricate, elaborate, and complex means of trying to get away with murder. Never mind that real-life criminals did not involve themselves in such unnatural tactics; the puzzle was the thing, and the goal of the author was to fool the reader.

The first variation on this theme began in the late 1920s and took over in the 1940s and early 1950s with the establishment of what came to be known as the private eye or hard-boiled school of detective fiction. It stemmed from an effort to bring realism into the mystery tale, to take murder "out of the bishop's rose garden and put it down in the gutter where it belongs." The detectives were no longer dilettantes, they were professionals who had to earn a living. The murderers stopped being evil geniuses with the time, patience, and wherewithal to concoct convoluted schemes of wickedness. Luck replaced skill on the villain's side to help confound the detective. While the puzzle remained intact and the author continued to try to misdirect the reader and produce a least-suspected murderer, the emphasis of the story shifted from puzzle to action. These tales were supposed to be interesting reads even for those who did not care about whodunit.

The best-known practitioners of the private eye school were Dashiell Hammett and Raymond Chandler, but many writers practiced the style and the variations on the theme were multiple. There were loners like Hammett's Sam Spade, Chandler's Philip Marlowe, Brett Halliday's Mike Shayne, and ultimately, Mickey Spillane's Mike Hammer. There were also cute young couples like Frances and Richard Lockridge's Mr. and Mrs. North, James Fox's John and Suzy Marshall, and Delano Ames's Jane and Dagobert Brown.

Although the classical and private eye detectives operated in widely disparate environments and in radically different ways, both shared certain traits. Both, for example, were virtually free of legal restraint. Both, for whatever reason, were laws unto themselves. Both operated alone and kept their own counsel.

While the private eye school might appear realistic in contrast to the classical school, it was a far cry from reality and grew steadily farther as the hard-boiled school degenerated into the sex-and-sadism school. Where Hammett's Nick Charles nipped at the bottle because he and Nora were on vacation in New York, later detectives came to live almost entirely on Scotch, suffering not the slightest impairment of their faculties. Where Sam Spade startled mystery readers by going to bed with a lady client and having an affair with his partner's wife, later detectives encountered a female population consisting almost totally of beautiful blond nymphomaniacs.

The police procedural can be regarded as a revolt against the hardboiled school and a new attempt to bring realism to the mystery novel. The police procedural, as its name implies, attempted to show "real" policemen solving "real" crimes in the manner that crimes "really" are solved. It was, as a result, radically different from the other two forms. The police procedural thrust the detective into the middle of a working police force, full of rules and regulations. Instead of bypassing the police, the procedural took readers inside the department and showed them how it worked.

These are stories not just about police but about the world of the police. Police Inspector Charlie Chan doesn't belong, for there are no police in his world. Inspector Maigret doesn't belong. Although there are police in his stories, they are not a factor.

When we speak of police procedurals, we're talking about the 87th Precinct novels of Ed McBain, the Elizabeth Linington–Dell Shannon–Lesley Egan novels about the Glendale and Los Angeles police. There

are John Creasey's Inspector West and Gideon series and the Per Wah-
loo and Maj Sjowall tales about Martin Beck. These are stories about
big-city police forces. In the area of the small-town procedural, there
may be none other than my own Chief Fred Fellows.

The birth of the police procedural might be worth my pausing to
reflect for a moment, since I was one of those involved in it.

Lawrence Treat is acknowledged to be the first mystery writer to
have professional policemen, shown in a police environment, solve a
crime with authentic police methods. This was in his book *V as in
Victim*, published in 1945. It would not be proper, however, to call
him the father of the police procedural, for he was ahead of his time.
There was no rush to follow his lead. In fact, the next effort in that
direction appears to have been the movie *Naked City*, which came out
in 1948.

My own involvement commenced in 1949 and had no connection
with either event. What happened was that after a series of three cute-
young-couple detective stories, I chanced upon a slim paperback en-
titled *They All Died Young* by Charles Boswell, which was a collection
of ten true murder cases in which the victims were young women. I
read the stories one by one, and they totally changed my approach to
the mystery novel. These tales had a vividness and a horror unlike any
mystery fiction I had either written or read.

Immediately, I wanted to get that same sense of shock and horror
into my own fiction, and I set about analyzing the cause of their impact.
The obvious answer was that these murders weren't make-believe; they
had really happened. One of the victims, in fact, had been a nurse in
my home city who'd had her throat cut and had collapsed and died on
the hospital steps. The question was, How do we know these cases are
true, other than the author's say-so? The answer: Because they sound
that way. I decided that the quality that gave these stories their brutal
ugliness was their ring of authenticity. The stories affected me not
because the author said they really happened but because they read
that way.

I then determined to write a fictional murder mystery that would
sound as if it had really happened. Since it is not private eyes and cute
young couples who solve real murders, or hard-boiled private eyes, or
dilettante detectives, but sheriffs, police chiefs, and police detectives,
I had to take a totally new approach to the art of mystery writing.

That is what I promptly did. The year was 1950, and the story was about the murder of a young college student, solved, as in real life, through the efforts of those whose business it really is, the professional police. So far as I knew—being unaware of Treat's book—no one had done it before.

Apparently, the time for the police procedural had come. Not only was I turning in that direction, others were as well. By the time my novel *Last Seen Wearing* . . . was published in late 1952, the radio program *Dragnet* had come into being and enjoyed great success. In fact, if anything can be called the father of the police procedural, it might be that program, for while no procedural writer I have talked to points to *Dragnet* as a source of inspiration, most not having written their first procedural until long after the program's demise, I would regard it as inevitable that the potential of the police station background was first brought to their attention by Sergeant Joe Friday and company.

This business of moving toward the police instead of away, as in the first two forms of the detective story, separates them from the procedural and gives the writer of procedurals a different set of problems than the writers of the classical and private eye tales. Let us consider them in detail.

The suspension of disbelief—meaning how much unreality the reader will endure before saying "This is ridiculous!"—varies according to the type of tale being told. Readers will accept witches, magic spells, and gingerbread houses in fairy tales but would reject machine guns and electric lights in Civil War novels. A great deal of realism is demanded of the procedural.

Consider the classical detective story. The villains in those tales, in order to be worthy foes of the superintelligent detective, had to devise incredibly clever plots. The authors invented puzzles that were exquisite pieces of intellectual architecture. Such mysteries could not pretend to represent reality. Real-life murders aren't that elaborately planned. Most actual killings are, in fact, spur-of-the-moment impulses with barely enough advance thought to do more than justify the term "premeditation." In real life the hardest crime to solve is not the one in which every detail has been worked out months in advance but the unwitnessed, spur-of-the-moment murder wherein the victim was unknown to the assailant, as in the case of rape or robbery.

Such real-life occurrences wouldn't fit the puzzle structure of the classical detective story. Since puzzle was the purpose, reality had to be sacrificed, and the reader was willing to suspend disbelief.

In the interests of the puzzle, other realities were also overlooked, and so the classical detective story was structured in a language all its own. Numerous artificial devices were uncritically accepted as proper baggage. Most notable was the traditional denouement in which all the suspects were gathered together and the detective proceeded to point a finger at one after another, maintaining suspense at its maximum, until he finally pointed out the villain and explained in detail how he had found him or her out. Never mind that this is the last thing a real detective would do; the requisite of the puzzle story demanded it.

Another device was the detective's habit of keeping all the threads of the mystery in his own head, committing nothing to paper, confiding in no one. Keeping the reader in the dark required this approach. It also provided the writer with an easy suspense gimmick, for it made the detective a tempting target for the villain.

Certain artificialities in the form of clues became acceptable. These were not, however, born of necessity but of ignorance and were due to the fact that the mystery writers of that era did not bother with the police or make any effort to verify their suppositions. Thus it was accepted as gospel in such novels that fingerprints abound and are readily discoverable on guns. As an adjunct, it was accepted that fingerprints would be protected rather than smudged if the gun was wrapped in a handkerchief. The facts of the matter are that an identifiable fingerprint is hard to come by, even on such receptive surfaces as mirrors and glassware, and the chances of obtaining a print from a gun are very nearly zero.

Other bits of misinformation which the writers of the era used as clues were that the expression on the victim's face revealed his or her emotion (fear, surprise, etc.) at the moment of death, that pathologists could determine almost to the minute how long the victim had been dead, and that headless corpses could easily be misidentified.

None of this is true, of course. The best that can be said of the face of a corpse is that it has no expression. As for times of death, so many variables affect the onset of postmortem changes that an accurate determination is almost impossible without the help of additional evidence. And of course, the means of identification of bodies by other than facial characteristics are plentiful. However, for purposes of the puzzle, these gospels of ignorance helped the authors with their clue planting, and readers learned to accept them. The astute reader, for instance, would immediately know that any corpse with a missing head or damaged face belonged to someone else and that in all likelihood the supposed victim was really the murderer.

Nor did the killers in these tales ever take the Fifth Amendment or deny the accusation, safe in the assurance that there was insufficient formal evidence to convict them. Such a concession to realism would make for inconclusive endings, and that would never do. Murderers, for one reason or another, had to confess in the interests of tidiness. When the puzzle ended, the book had to end.

The private eye school, in its efforts to increase realism, altered some of these procedures. The plots weren't as intricate, and the answers were hidden from the reader by an overlay of action rather than intellectual obfuscation. Writers in this area avoided some of the grosser errors regarding fingerprints and other clues and, for that matter, used fewer of such clues, perhaps feeling themselves on unsure ground. Still and all, the private eye tale was rife with unrealities. The detective customarily arrived on the murder scene ahead of the police, tampered with evidence, pocketed clues, and broke laws with a recklessness that could be justified only by the fact that the police in these stories were such bumbling idiots that had the detective not taken matters into his own hands so cavalierly, the case never would have been solved.

With the advent of the police procedural, suspension of disbelief was reduced to a minimum. The main impact of the procedural has been its ring of authenticity. Life inside the squad room must be portrayed accurately, and police vocabulary and procedures must be represented properly.

Nevertheless, even with the police procedural, a certain suspension of disbelief is demanded of the reader. A certain amount of unreality must be accepted or there can be no story.

Consider first the narrow field of the small-town police procedural. Suppose an author of such a series can produce two novels a year, not an excessive output. In each, there must be one or more confounding murders to solve, problems that strain the resources of both the reader and the police department.

In reality, a town of ten to twenty thousand inhabitants, insulated and self-contained, unassaulted by the outside world, would not have a real, honest-to-goodness murder more than once a decade. That's no more than ten a century. Of those ten, the chances are that eight or nine would pose no problem. The police would know who did it ten minutes after they reached the scene, and it would only be a matter of arresting the culprit and notifying the prosecuting attorney.

Inasmuch as procedural writers aren't going to write about easily solved crimes, the stories they tell involve the one or two murders per century that would pose serious problems for the police. Such a writer is going to write about crimes of the century, except that these crimes will be happening in his small town twice a year.

If this seems against the odds, there is also the fact that the small town in question is fortunate enough to have a high-powered resident detective capable of cracking these challenging cases. That lengthens the odds still further.

What about the big-city procedural in which the writer is dealing with a metropolitan police force? In New York City, for example, there are, as of recent count, 1800 murders a year, enough to provide a surfeit of hard-to-solve cases for the author's detective.

That part of the tale may be true to life. Accurate also might be the rules and regulations by which the police abide. The jargon can be learned; the difference between a street cop and a book cop can be understood. In time, an interested writer who has permission to research can so familiarize himself with the workings of the world of real detectives that he will know their territory and the threats to their survival. He might guffaw at their in jokes, understand the way they think and why. His books may be, therefore, rigorously accurate in all details, except—

The real-life detective does not do his detecting like Sherlock Holmes. He may observe as Holmes observed (indeed, he is trained that way); he may put pieces of a puzzle together as well as Holmes (he has a lot of others helping him); with the aid of the police lab, he can analyze substances far better than Holmes—but this is not the way most real-life crimes are solved. The real-life murder is not solved by ratiocination, by the exercise of Hercule Poirot's little gray cells, but by the accumulation of information. Hundreds of people are questioned, and, bit by bit, pieces of information are gathered which ultimately reveal what happened.

That's the hard way.

The easy way is to have the information brought in to police head-quarters. Ask a chief of detectives how crimes are solved and he won't say, "Clues." He'll answer, "Informants," informants being persons who secretly bring information to the police in return for money, favors, or other benefits. There is an adage that a detective is only as good as his informants, and while that may take away some of a detective's glamor, it's very true.

To the procedural writer, this poses certain problems. One of the rules of the detective story is that there must be detection. In real life, an informant may drop by police headquarters at three o'clock in the morning to tell the detectives who committed yesterday's murder and why, but an author can't tell it that way in a book. He must make the detective discover this for himself through finding and fitting together clues. But in doing so, he is getting away from reality and into the reader's suspension of disbelief.

Let us contrast the heroes of the classical and private eye school with those of the police procedural.

The detectives of the classical period were all patterned after Sherlock Holmes, created as men of giant intellect towering over their fellows, with only the villain as a challenger.

The classical detective was separated from the crowd in other ways as well. Father Brown wore a habit; Nero Wolfe was an obese gourmet; Poirot and Charlie Chan were foreigners, Vance a dilettante, Wimsey a lord, and the early Ellery Queen, effete. These were efforts by the authors to make their detectives distinctive, as Doyle had made Holmes distinctive. The homage paid to these men and their freedom from the vicissitudes of life—family responsibilities, jobs to go to, bills to pay—made them enviable. They, like Holmes, were free of encumbrances, able to devote their great mental powers exclusively to righting the wrongs at hand.

The hero of the private eye novel was a different species, but he enjoyed the same standing. He was a puzzle solver, too, but was not content to sit and ponder. He was a man of energy who solved cases through action. Most of the private eye heroes, like the classical detectives, had more than a touch of the superman about them. They were tough, brave, resourceful, and, as we have noted before, a law unto themselves. They tended to be cavalier, even flamboyant. The qualities that separated them from the rest of the cast was their ability to operate in excess of everyone else, whether it was the alcohol they could absorb, the beatings they could take, the laws they could break, or the women they could handle. Like the classical detective, they could not help but earn the envy of the reader.

What happens, on the other hand, when an author tries to create a hero for a police procedural? He's immediately in trouble, for the attractive superman hero is denied him by the nature of the genre. Not only does realism require that the hero of the procedural be human rather than superhuman, so do the restrictions of his job and his obligations to society.

Consider first the small-town procedural. Who can be the protagonist of such a story? Not a handsome young cop who drinks a quart of Scotch for breakfast and has to fight his way past the bevy of blonds camped outside his door; not a handsome young cop, even if he doesn't drink or date; not a young cop at all, no matter who he is.

When it comes to solving serious crimes, the responsibility goes to the top men on the force, which means the chief of police and his detectives. We're talking about older men, men who are probably married and raising families, men who are struggling, balding, graying, unromantic, and ordinary.

What about big-city detectives? What kind of heroes can they be? In a city such as New York, a homicide detective is assigned to work with the squad detective who catches a given homicide. They two are in charge of the investigation, although many other detectives may help in various phases, interviewing everyone in an apartment building, for example. Lab technicians, pathologists, photographers, emergency service workers, and other functionaries may be resorted to, but these are information-gathering operations whose information will then be delivered to the detectives in charge. So the detective hero could well be a member of the homicide squad. However, the author has the same problems listed above. These men are older (the youngest member of the homicide squad of Manhattan North, when I was researching it, was thirty-six), will have families, do not drink heavily without getting drunk, and cannot get bashed on the skull without suffering a concussion.

So what can a procedural author do about creating a detective hero if he cannot have him attain a position of authority until he has passed his handsome dashing youth; if he can't dine on gourmet foods and know the right wines because he lives on a policeman's salary; if he has to get to work on time, obey the law, and go through all the red tape that real police do; if he has to turn over significant parts of the investigation to others and stay in the good graces of his superiors, the public, and the board of police commissioners?

Such a man can't help being drab and ordinary. No single-handedly walking into the nest of thieves for him. (That's what the SWAT team does.) No sneaking into the bad guy's apartment to find crucial evidence. (It's illegal.) No keeping to himself bits of vital information so that he can hog the limelight when he socks it to them at the end. (He'd probably get reduced in rank.)

What, then, are the tactics for producing memorable detectives under these circumstances? It's not as easy to do as when a writer has the license to invent as he pleases, but the opportunities are still plentiful. The family life of the detective can be explored, a possibility that didn't exist in the classical and private eye forms. The relationships of the men in the squad can be made to play an important part in the story, an aspect of the mystery that didn't exist when the detective hero stood head and shoulders above his associates.

In fact, the squad room can become the equivalent of a daytime serial setting, meaning that readers can get to know the people, their personalities, and their problems so well that they look forward to the next book as a chance to rejoin old friends.

The hero of the procedural is radically different from the hero of the other two forms, but the procedural probably offers a richer vein to mine.

Despite the differences in the form of the hero, it is in the area of background that the greatest disparity occurs between the police procedural and the other two forms of the mystery. In the classical and private eye forms, the author could get away with minimal research into police tactics and techniques or none at all. This was because there was little incentive.

The creators of the classical detectives did not need to know how the police operated, for the only function of the police was to take the murderer away at the end. Nor was there need for the private eye writers to research police methods. Since their heroes operated beyond the law, there was no need to know what the law was.

The police procedural is, of course, the reverse. To the author of a procedural, not only must police procedures be known but also the law. Even a rookie cop has been drilled in criminal law and knows what he can and cannot do as well as the requirements he must satisfy. The procedural writer can do no less and must dig into the laws of evidence and know how to cope with the *Miranda* decision.

The writer of a procedural has the problem of not only inventing a compelling story but of researching it thoroughly.

Lastly we must consider the story that takes place against this procedural background, and this poses interesting questions.

In both the classical and private eye story there was a puzzle to be solved and a villain to be caught; since the reader was engaged as a participant, there had to be fair play. The reader had to know everything the detective knew.

Does the puzzle exist in the procedural?

The answer is yes. But depending on the type of procedural, it can be foremost, as in the small-town procedural where nothing else is happening, or as low as third fiddle in the big-city tale, coming in behind both action and background.

It still, however, must be there. The mystery cannot solve itself or, as mentioned earlier, be solved by the unsolicited arrival of an informant. The detectives must work at a solution, and the solution must result from their work.

There is one notable difference, however, in the way in which the solution is undertaken. That is in the matter of the fair fight.

In the classical school, it was important that the talents of the genius detective be tested properly. Thus, the villains were endowed with comparable skills, and the battle between detective and murderer was between evenly matched opponents. The detective, in order to earn the mantle of greatness, had to best the best. This is why the puzzles he had to unravel were so elaborate, why the murderers were so clever, why all the odds had to be stacked in the opponent's favor. Chance could not solve the case for the detective. It could only operate on behalf of the villain, making the detective's problem more difficult.

In like manner, the private eye had to outwit the gang leader and usually had to overcome, single-handedly, not just the leader but his minions. The odds again were stacked against the detective.

With the police procedural, we find that the reverse is true. Instead of the odds favoring the bad guy, they now favor the forces of law and order. Against the murderer, who not only is not a genius but is probably of below-average intelligence, we can count on two detectives working full time toward his apprehension while, behind them, at their beck and call, lie the total resources of the police, medical, and legal systems of the community. Let the villain hole up in an abandoned warehouse, and he won't face the hero in a one-to-one battle. He'll be up against a team of men, all of them more heavily armed, skilled, and protected than he is. They will have tear gas, searchlights, walkie-talkies, helicopters—an awesome array of tools that produces a total mismatch. It's enough to make the reader sympathize with the villain instead of the hero.

Whether the reader actually cares about this shift in the odds is uncertain. Nevertheless, it is a factor which I consider important, and in my books I see to it that the heavy police superiority is overcome and a fair fight situation reestablished. My tactic is to create stories in which all the advantages the detective enjoys fail to flush the criminal from cover. When all else comes to naught, it is the hero's wits and skill, pitted against the odds favoring the villain, that finally unmask the villain.

The police procedural is, to me, a more demanding and challenging type of detective story than either the classical or the private eye genre. I find it, however, much more rewarding.

4

The Whydunit Emerges, Thanks to Freud

Lucy Freeman

The revolutionary theories of Freud about the human mind have affected almost every area of life and the mystery novel and fact-crime book are no exception. Freud's discovery that the act of murder has its origin in the nursery has added an important dimension both to novels about murder and to true stories about killers.

A new genre, dubbed the "whydunit," has arisen which, in addition to the suspense built up in discovering "who" committed the murder, also reveals what in the person's past inexorably compelled him or her to kill.

The whydunit gives the reader the added thrill of understanding and identifying more closely with the motives of the murderer. While such crimes may seem to spring out of current conflicts—hatred of a wife or husband, an old wealthy aunt or uncle, or a business partner—they are sparked by childhood hatreds relating to the mother and father. We all have murderous wishes in childhood because we are bound to feel angry at parents who frustrate us, as they must at times while we learn to be "civilized." Luckily, most of us have loving parents, and so we do not act on the murderous wishes of childhood. But we read about how others murder, giving their repressed childhood wishes an explosive outlet. Those who merely read allow angry wishes a temporary, safe outlet—probably the chief reason for the popularity of murder mysteries.

The successful writer, both in fiction and in fact-crime, does not explain the murderer's past in the clinical terms of psychoanalytic truths but in the artful fashion of imaginative style, dramatic form, and characterization.

Take Robert Bloch's classic *Psycho*, first published in 1959, then made by Hitchcock into a movie still seen regularly on television. It is one of the top moneymakers of all time, made, alas, before writers asked for their fair share of profits.

The chief character, Norman Bates, is sensitively played by Anthony Perkins (before he himself entered psychoanalysis, which, he has said publicly, benefited him immensely). Norman is an outwardly affable young man living with his mother in a ghostlike house on the top of a hill in a Texas town near Dallas. Norman manages the tourist cabins below, which bring in money for his mother and him to live on.

One evening Mary Crane drives up to the cabins for an overnight stay. She has stolen $40,000 from her employer so she can marry Sam Loomis, who plans to join her in Dallas, not knowing of the theft. Mary undresses, preparing for a night's sleep, then decides to take a shower. As she steps naked into the bathroom, a hooded figure creeps into her cabin.

Suddenly she sees a face peering through the bathtub curtain. A scarf conceals the hair, glassy eyes stare at her "inhumanly." The face is powdered dead-white and spots of rouge dot each cheek. Then she realizes: "It wasn't a mask. It was the face of a crazy old woman."

Mary starts to scream, the curtains part, and a hand lunges at her, wielding a butcher knife. In the words of the author, "It was the knife that, a moment later, cut off her scream.

"And her head."

Thus the famous bathroom murder scene. Followed by other murders as Sam Loomis, the bereaved fiancé, and Mary's sister Lila set out to find the lost woman, sensing she has come to a dreadful end.

Along the way Bloch skillfully plants psychological clues about the identity of the murderer and the reasons for the crime, taking the reader into Norman's mind. After he murders Mary, for instance, Norman sits in the office drinking to steady his nerves, dreaming of Mary naked in the bathroom. He thinks:

"Funny, when he actually saw her, he had this terrible feeling of— what was the word? *Im*-something. *Im*portance. No, that wasn't it. He didn't feel important when he was with a woman. He felt—*im*possible? That wasn't right, either. He knew the word he was looking for, he'd read it a hundred times in books, the kind of books Mother didn't even know he owned. . . . Well, it didn't matter. When he was with the girl he felt that way, but not now. Now he could do anything."

He remembers the word when he thinks again of the dead girl, wishing that he had offered her a drink and then carried her to the bed. The word is "impotent."

In one of the final scenes, as Norman tries to kill Lila, he is revealed as the murderer. She opens the door of the fruit cellar and sees what she believes is an old woman lying there, the wrinkled face grinning up at her "in an obscene greeting." It is the skeleton of the mother.

There is a second figure hidden in the fruit cellar, a live figure, wearing a woman's dress over a man's trousers and shirt. His face is painted garishly in woman's makeup. The figure raises a knife to kill Lila.

The voice that emerges from the figure is high and shrill as the figure says, "*I am Norma Bates.*"

Sam Loomis rushes in and twists the knife from the murderer's hand before he is able to strike Lila. There is a scream from the murderer: "It was the insane scream of a hysterical woman, and it came from the throat of Norman Bates."

The psychiatrist called in to examine Norman explains that as a boy Norman had been kept excessively close to his mother, a dominating, jealous woman who did not want him to marry or leave her side. In his identification with his mother, he became a transvestite. When his mother, a widow, suddenly decided to marry again, Norman killed both her and her suitor. But he kept her body in the house, dressing her skeleton in clothes, and sometimes sat her at the window so guests thought they saw a live person.

He literally took over her personality, psychologically merging with her. When he felt sexually attracted to a woman, he became the jealous mother, getting rid of the rival her son desired. His impotence was the result of fear of his mother and unnatural attachment to her.

Here Freud's oedipal conflict is sensitively portrayed as well as another of his theories—that of the early fusion of the child with the mother. This merging is part of the fantasy of the infant's first months, before he starts to see himself as separate from the mother. But if she does not allow him to separate emotionally from her, he will feel he *is* her in many respects. He will hate her, for when a mother thwarts a child's natural psychosexual development toward independence, the child will resent not achieving an identity. He is caught in the dilemma of needing to retain her love so she will feed him and of giving in to her excessive demands and restrictions. Later in life, as an adult, the emotionally crippled child may take revenge by killing substitute targets.

As Norman Bates says, "To know that you are real—that's sanity, isn't it?" Norman never felt "real," too dependent on a very emotionally disturbed mother to move into the world of reality. Bloch takes us into the fantasies that prevented Norman from being sane, fantasies that drove him to kill because he was still under the obsessive sway of a jealous, overpossessive mother.

Then there is Stanley Ellin's *Mirror, Mirror on the Wall* (1972). To summarize this book is difficult; it has to be read to grasp its powerful story and shocking denouement. Ellin also takes us inside the mind of a man possessed by his past, a past that drives him to murder. It involves a seductive father with whom he is in competition, which rouses feelings of envy and hate; yet he wants to keep his father's love. This is the dilemma all children must resolve in regard to the parent of the same sex as they prepare to transfer erotic and tender love to an appropriate person outside the family. Those original family ties are very strong, however, and a number of men and women never succeed in breaking them.

The child-parent emotions that can haunt one to the point of eventual murder also appear in Gregory Mcdonald's *Running Scared* (1964), though it is concerned not with actual murder but failure to prevent a suicide. The story opens as Thomas Betancourt, son of a wealthy New York lawyer, does nothing to stop his nineteen-year-old roommate at a university from slashing his wrists and bleeding to death. He believes it was his roommate's right to kill himself if he was suffering.

Tom becomes involved in a love affair with the dead boy's sister and slowly realizes why he did not try to stop his roommate's death. Tom does not believe in love, as he explains to Sarah, a girl with whom he has sex and who wants to marry him but whom he cannot love, "Love is a weakness. . . . When you love, you are vulnerable."

He finally acknowledges the feeling of love with his dead roommate's sister, and this leads to his destruction. His lack of emotional involvement with a woman was a defense against his destructive feelings for a man with whom his mother had been having an eight-year affair. Tom realizes that if he had not deadened his feelings of love for his mother, he would have killed this man because of his own strong incestuous feelings. When he has to face the intensity of both his love and his hate, it becomes unbearable, and he unconsciously destroys himself. *Running Scared* is an apt title for the story of his emotional life.

According to Freud and later psychoanalysts, our two strongest drives, sex and aggression, become "fused" to a moderate degree as we develop emotionally. But if parents do not provide enough love and emotional security, if they are brutally cruel, if they have not really wanted a child, this fusion fails to take place and an intense aggressive drive, not tempered by compassion and love, may lead to murder or other destructive behavior, such as addiction, proneness to accidents, psychosomatic illnesses, or deep depression.

How the outright cruelty of a parent, especially as it affects normal sexual development and feelings of hate, may create a murderer is shown by Dave Klein in the recent *Blind Side* (1980), an impressive first novel. Klein depicts a football player compulsively driven to murder prostitutes, and we try to figure out which member of the team is the killer.

The story involves a son unconsciously carrying out his mother's wish that he murder the "loose women" with whom his father is perpetually involved. In vivid flashbacks, without letting us know which player is the criminal, Klein portrays the cruelty his mother inflicted on him as a boy of twelve:

> "ohgodohgod it hurts!
> "Why?
> "Crack!
> "He could hear the leather strap whistling as it cut through the air. It seemed to take a long time before it struck. . . . It exploded, again, biting into flesh, flaying skin, hurrying thick drops of blood welling up to the surface. . . . He bit down on his lower lip, teeth almost embedded, so that he wouldn't scream and show that it hurt. . . .
> "He was slipping, sliding, falling; the pain was his only anchor. . . ."

His Bible-quoting mother had beaten him almost unconscious because she caught him masturbating. She had tied his hands with a rope to the bale hook on the wall of the barn after thrashing him and then ordered him not to tell his father. He had slumped to the ground, into the straw and dirt, thinking, "*I hate you, Momma. Hate you. Hate you. Some day . . . some day, Momma, I'm gonna kill you, Momma.*" And when he was big and strong, he killed both her and his promiscuous father with whom she also had sex, which made her "bad." And he killed dozens of other "bad women" as he rose to national fame with the triumphant Panthers football team.

This explosive, original psychosexual suspense story explores in depth the origin of murder. Klein, a sportswriter who knows his Freud, also knows that a mother who beats her son for masturbating not only creates this special trauma but can offer a son little emotional sustenance.

In the 1940s, Robert Paul Smith, who wrote the sensitive children's book *Where Did You Go? Out. What Did You Do? Nothing?*, also wrote a murder mystery, *Because of My Love*. It is the story of a daughter's attachment to a very seductive father whom she eventually murders, as she also does her husband. Both are men she fears and yearns for, who, in the childhood fantasy that still grips her, are illicit lovers who have seduced her. This creates an unbearable sense of guilt which she can relieve only by getting rid of them.

In Graham Greene's *Brighton Rock* (1938), the psychopathic young killer's early childhood in the slums with brutal parents is described eloquently as Greene provides a psychological understanding of the roots of murder.

There are writers who have used a psychiatrist or psychoanalyst as sleuth, including myself. In *The Dream*, I showed how a psychoanalyst tracks down the murderer of his patient, a publisher, through the latter's dream, which the patient recounted during his final session on the couch. A dream shows in symbolic form the existence of a current conflict connected with a conflict of the past. The hero-analyst is able to decipher the dream and discover whom the patient fears most in his current life; then he obtains a confession from the killer.

In the world of true-crime books there have been several bestsellers that show the connection between a murderer and the cruelty inflicted on him as a child. One of the first in this country was Dr. Fredric Wertham's *Dark Legend* (1941). When he wrote it, Wertham, who died recently, was director of the Psychiatric Service of Queens General

Hospital, New York, and director of Lafargue Clinic and the Readjustment Center, Quaker Emergency Service, New York.

Wertham, in what he calls his own "detective case," searched not for the murderer but the motive as he tried to understand why a seventeen-year-old boy, Gino, from one of New York's crowded tenement sections in the Lower East Side, killed his mother. The crime made headlines for a few days and then was forgotten, except by Dr. Wertham, who had first examined Gino. To Wertham, the boy was a pitiful and appealing figure. As Wertham embarked on his quest for clues as to the motives, a remarkable and moving tale emerged.

The story starts as an Italian boy of average height, slim, with black hair and expressive brown eyes, walks out of a candy store and up to a policeman. The policeman notices that one of the boy's hands is wrapped clumsily in a white handkerchief and blood is seeping through it.

"Cut yourself?" asks the policeman.

"Yeah," says the boy. He leans a little closer to the policeman; his brown eyes look directly into the policeman's eyes, and he says, "Yeah. I just killed my mother."

He had slashed his mother with a bread knife. His father had been dead several years, leaving Gino with a younger brother and several sisters. He worked, gave his mother money to take care of the family. He told Dr. Wertham he had killed his mother "because she dishonored my family." There had been another man in her life after her husband's death.

Gino was committed to a state asylum for the criminally insane on Dr. Wertham's recommendation. The case was closed for the police but for Dr. Wertham "the mystery had merely begun."

A petition from thirty-one of Gino's neighbors, spontaneously drawn up after the crime and sent to the authorities, described Gino as a hard worker, scrupulously honest, "of good and high moral feelings, of clean habits, and never associated with people of dubious character." Gino told Dr. Wertham, "I killed my mother. I took her life away. But no one can say I ever disobeyed her."

His mother had promised his dying father not to marry again but then became sexually involved with his father's brother. Gino himself had never had a girl; he was deeply attached to his mother. He had consoled her when his father died, felt he must guard her from other men. When he killed her, Dr. Wertham said, Gino unconsciously felt he was doing what his father wished him to do—protect the family honor and keep his mother faithful to his father's memory. He was punishing his mother for her unfaithfulness, as Orestes had done in the Greek myth.

Wertham said he knew there was a deeper motive than revenge for family honor. That was the conscious motive. What was the unconscious motive, the hidden motive?

Wertham set about to find it. He had studied sons with an obsessive fear of injuring their mothers with sharp instruments and found in each case that the fear "was the result of a profound emotional conflict based on an unusually strong attachment to the mother." Gino's mother had been his "stern educator" when he was little, emphasizing cleanliness, neatness, and obedience by often beating him severely. He had known violence at her hands and also seduction, though she had stopped kissing him after his father died, as though the protective barrier for her own feelings had been removed.

Wertham also found that Gino was afraid of his erotic feelings for his young mother, who was only sixteen when he was born. One day he sneaked home and surprised his mother and uncle in sexual intimacy. He hated her for being unfaithful to him. His fantasy life, in Dr. Wertham's words, "had a red thread running through it: incest and the dread of incest." Gino wanted his mother sexually and could not bear the thought that another man was enjoying sex with her.

Wertham explains: "I felt that I had now come near the truth. Gino wanted to kill his mother not in spite of his love for her, but because of it. . . . He could not run away because he loved his mother and could not leave her. The mother-image, loved and hated at the same time, overshadowed all his life. It had to be destroyed."

Gino had murdered the mother who in his fantasy had been untrue to him after accepting him as his father's substitute and allowing him to believe she loved him alone. One very important factor which Wertham does not emphasize but later psychiatrists would is that she was the instigator of violence in the family. Had she not beaten him severely when he was a boy, he would not have acquired the taste for the violence that ultimately caused her death.

One of the more recent studies of murderers is Truman Capote's *In Cold Blood* (1966), in which he describes how the wanton killings committed by two men originated in their brutal childhoods. Probably the most penetrating study of a murderer yet written is a book by Flora Rheta Schreiber, as yet untitled, which follows her famous *Sybil.* She delves into the past—including the first tortured days of his life— of Joseph Kallinger, a Philadelphia shoemaker found guilty of murdering a nurse in Leonia, New Jersey. It is expected to be published in late 1982.

In addition to her career as professor at John Jay College of Criminal Justice of the City of New York, Flora spent a good part of the past six years writing the book and interviewing Kallinger in a Pennsylvania prison. She became his friend, gained his trust, almost served as his psychoanalyst as he spoke freely to her of a childhood unbelievably traumatic, containing physical abuse and threats of castration by foster parents as well as sexual abuse by peers.

In describing Kallinger's fantasies, hallucinations, and tragic life, Flora demonstrates many of Freud's theories of sexuality and aggression. Her book is testimony not only to what Freud discovered but to her art as a dramatic writer and her intuitive ability to grasp the relationship between the emotional nurturing necessary for the healthy mental development of a child and the act of murder.

There is plenty of proof of Freud's theories, though it is never clinical but rather always within the characterization and action in this study of Joseph Kallinger. For instance, he cannot have sex with his wife unless there is a knife under the pillow. And he uses the knife to kill. The knife, representing the phallus, is at hand for reassurance in the case of his wife, whom he does not fear. But with a woman he fears, a stranger, he must use the knife instead of the phallus, for he is afraid of being impotent and blames the woman.

Incidentally, a creative writer needs no personal experience with psychoanalysis to understand Freud's theories. When Robert Bloch was asked how long he had been in analysis before writing *Psycho*, he said, "I've never been to a psychoanalyst." Neither has Flora, though she did write a mental health column with Melvin Herman for several years.

The understanding of psychological motivation also appears in many contemporary short stories, such as Helen McCloy's "The Other Side of the Curtain," in which a woman's dream is finally seen as reality when she realizes her husband has trapped her into being convicted of a murder he planned; and Eleanor Sullivan's "Something Like Growing Pains," about a severely depressed wife who stares at a husband who continually tears her down and thinks: "Why did I marry him? Why did he marry me? What made us think we could be happy?" She then chooses a way to end the misery for both. Emotional maturity is hard come by, but in Gloria Amoury's "Come into My Parlor," an ex-wife stalks for years the woman who had taken her perfect husband from her. After he dies, the ex-wife confronts the other woman, only to learn he had made her utterly miserable—a side of him she had never seen. She decides to look within to find out why she had chosen him in the first place.

Partly as a result of Freud's opening the door to greater freedom in the discussion of sexuality, the mystery novel has become threaded through with sexual scenes. Some sleuths are more Don Juans than astute detectives. After all, the only thing better than vicariously enjoying murderous feelings is vicariously enjoying sexual feelings. When you combine the two, you hit the suspense jackpot.

In Ken Follett's *Eye of the Needle* (1980), the love affair between the German spy, Henry Faber, and Mrs. Lucy Rose makes the book different from most spy stories. Faber, whose code name is "the Needle," after his favorite weapon, the stiletto, which he uses to silence anyone who gets in his way, has been planted in London to discover where the Allies plan their D-Day landing. He and Lucy fall in love as he feels tenderness toward a woman for the first time. As he tries to get off the storm-battered island where Lucy and her crippled husband live, a duel of wits takes place when Lucy learns Henry has discovered the invasion plan and intends to transmit it to Hitler. The spy loses his life because he is unable to kill her, and she kills him.

In the old days, if the hero bestowed a chaste kiss on a woman's cheek, that was considered daring. His business was to solve the crime, not dally with a dame in the bedroom.

But today:

"You're so beautiful," he said, kissing her forehead, eyes, nose, lips, neck, lips moving lower, between her breasts, then the nipples, and then taking the nipples between his lips, feeling them swell and swell, his tongue circling the tips, his lips gently sucking, until her body began to vibrate ever so slightly and her breath quickened.

She was kissing him then, her hands touching him, her lips and fingers

caressing his body, arousing him more, until she became a part of him, he
became a part of her. Then:

"Oh—God!" she whispered joyously. "Oh—"

This is a scene from *The Diamond Exchange* (1981), a Max Kauffman
novel by Thomas Chastain. Diamonds are definitely not a girl's best
friend, even in a suspense story.

In *Blind Side*, author Dave Klein has a climactic scene involving
sex of the most brutal nature, calculated to stir many emotions. It is
original and daring and fits the character of the murderer. To para-
phrase Freud, when the aggressive impulse dominates the love impulse,
what comes out is not tenderness and thoughtfulness but rape and
brutality.

As in Faulkner's *Sanctuary* (1931), where the rape of Temple Drake
is the crime, there is sex but no love. Faulkner later explains in graphic
detail why the rapist, Popeye, is impotent and has to use a corncob.
Even a Nobel Prize winner, decades ago, was using Freud to explain
sexual aberrations.

Thus a number of current writers of mysteries are aware of what
has become known by psychoanalysts as the "preoedipal period." This
is the first few years of life, when the child's relationship is primarily
to the mother as she either cares for him adequately or enrages him so
that murder remains in his heart.

Current writers are portraying psychological truths so honestly
and artistically that the truths are brought home to the reader with
greater conviction than in textbooks. One recent example is Joyce Har-
rington's *Family Reunion* (1982), which starts out, "Sometimes at night
I dream of River House, standing alone on the only high ground for
miles around above the rushing brown water," and then slowly, inexorably, leads the reader into a psychic labyrinth of murder and suspense
that is stunning.

Such writing extends the knowledge of the motives for murder to
many readers. It makes Freud's powerful theories more relevant than
ever.

That is the goal sublime—to entertain and to enrich in knowledge,
especially knowledge of the self—a goal achieved today by many mystery writers as they create on paper the suspense that exists both in
the outer world, where murder is rampant, and in the inner lives of
their characters.

5

Murder in Mother Goose?
Helen Wells

Theft in Mother Goose?

"Tom, Tom, the piper's son,
Stole a pig and away he run!"

Murder in Mother Goose?

"Who killed Cock Robin?
I, said the sparrow,
With my bow and arrow.
I killed Cock Robin."

At every age of life, starting in the nursery, suspense, mysteries, and tales of wonder arouse a delicious fear and curiosity. As those scholars of the mystery story Chris Steinbrunner and Otto Penzler note in their *Detectionary* (1976): "Mystery fiction has a history almost as long as literature itself. Enthusiasts are known in every country, at every social level."

Even the youngest readers respond to the sound of excited voices telling a mystery. The youngest ones look at the illustrations that convey as much of the story as the simple, songlike texts. *A Dark, Dark Tale*, written and illustrated by Ruth Brown, creates suspense in a dark castle where a gentle black cat explores to find—surprise! Another imaginative and richly illustrated suspense tale for the very young is *The Garden of Abdul Gasazi* by C. Van Allsburg.

The so-called little kids, ages four to seven, have a mystery literature of their own. Reprinted many times is *Chameleon Was a Spy* by Diane Redfield Massie. It's about an enterprising, small green chameleon who climbs into a bottle of pickles and thereby discovers and steals the tasty recipe. It won a Scroll Award in 1977 from the Mystery Writers of America as one of the year's best juvenile mystery stories.

For the next older age group, children from six to nine, *Funnyman's First Case* by Stephen Mooser is an amusing read. *Nate the Great and the Missing Key* by Marjorie Sharmat is engaging, disarming, and ridiculous. Nate the Great, of course, is the small boy detective in the case (he can't find his front door key), innocently outwitted by his dog.

Elizabeth Levy's *Frankenstein Moved in on the Fourth Floor*, told by a baffled eight-year-old boy explaining the case to his younger brother, is a classic of big-city humor, believable and genuinely mystifying.

More complex and realistic mysteries are written, often with humor, for kids eight to twelve. Witty, loving, and downright funny is *Happles and Cinnamunger* by Mary Francis Shura. The "haunts"—poltergeists—come to the kids' house with scary and mystifying results. Another that is real fun for readers eight to twelve is *The Case of the Crooked Kids* by Terrence Dicks. Avi's *Who Stole the Wizard of Oz?*, for readers eight to twelve is great fun and a tantalizing mystery, more imaginative than most.

A happy surprise for children eight to twelve is *The Young Detective's Handbook* by William Vivian Butler. It's a thoroughly competent how-to book with lively examples. The handbook repeatedly warns the young would-be detective not to tangle with criminals himself but simply to supply information to the police.

For readers twelve to sixteen, the young adults, or YAs, there's a lively and sizable publishing segment. Mystery novels written for YAs often have so much substance that in some cases they are reissued for adults.

In short, the twentieth-century boom in the mystery story has spread to young readers, too. At New York's book fair, young children are brought by their parents, and teenagers wander around in groups of their own, with mystery titles getting a full share of attention.

Juvenile mysteries parallel the adult mysteries—mystery, suspense, detection, fantasy, occult, science fiction—and at the same time create distinctively juvenile categories, especially young detectives. Edward D. Hoch writes: "The best juvenile mysteries are those which are good mysteries first of all, and juveniles second. Mystery Writers of America's Edgar Awards nominees (Edgar for Edgar Allan Poe), for the best juvenile mystery of each year, all have strong plots, and characters the young readers can identify with."

A prime question in all mystery stories is, Who is the detective? For the youngest readers, sometimes it's an animal such as Robert Quackenbush's Detective Mole or Peter Pack Rat. Eve Titus's four Basil of Baker Street books feature a mouse detective that "learned its trade at the feet of Sherlock Holmes." The mouse will head a TV series to be produced by Disney.

But animal characters are not as popular as they used to be, and such stories depend on humor along with mystery. I prefer Robert Quackenbush's series about Piet Potter, a very young New York City amateur detective based on the author's small son, Piet.

In Mary Blount Christian's hilariously illustrated *Two-Ton Secret*, a self-appointed detective and his assistant ($1 per case) slide down a pile of dirt and thereby discover a key clue to the puzzle of a missing bulldozer.

Private eyes in juvenile mysteries now range in age from six to eight, as in Joan Lowery Nixon's Edgar-winning *The Mysterious Red Tape Gang*. These little kids, observing some strange goings-on in their neighborhood and seeing one of the fathers badly worried, figure out what the bad guys are up to and foil them. Even at age six you can let the air out of all the tires on the crook's car so that the police can get there in time and foil his getaway.

For readers age eight to twelve, teams of two or more young detectives are cropping up. In *Black Magic at Brillstone*, the Heides, a mother-daughter writing partnership, send Liza and Logan to the rescue.

The old series favorites have youthful detectives who in their late teens or early twenties are much older than their readers. Several generations have read and continue to read the Hardy Boys, Nancy Drew, Cherry Ames (reissued as *The Case of the Forgetful Patient*, *The Case of the Dangerous Remedy*, *Mystery of Rogue's Cave*, etc), Trixie Belden, and the Bobbsey Twins. These are straightforward detection with a variety of backgrounds, adventure, and romance.

A new series for children eight to twelve has the overall title *Alfred*

Hitchcock and the Three Investigators, who are three young boys. One of the newest and best in this series is *Mystery of the Blazing Cliffs* by M. V. Carey. Each book comes with a mystery quiz and a bookmark.

In contrast, young adult books are focusing less on detectives and mystery than on psychological themes. Many readers begin to read adult mysteries at age fourteen or fifteen. Many read adult novels along with YA novels, which deal with their own problems: the discomfort and bewilderment of growing up, changing family relationships, peer and teacher relationships in junior high and high school, competition in sports and dating, self-doubt, changes in one's body and one's feelings. With one foot in childhood yet approaching adult status, these readers demand serious and honest novels in which the mystery is only one element.

It's no accident that in young adult nonfiction Arnold Madison (still young himself) has written hard-hitting books: *Drugs and You*, *Runaway Teens*, and *Suicide and Young People*. Of his fiction, which includes an MWA Scroll Award for *Danger Beats the Drum*, Mr. Madison comments: "Juvenile mysteries have grown up in the last few years. Gone, thank heavens, are the books where children spent 120 pages searching for a diamond ring only to discover the friendly crow in the apple tree stole the jewelry. Serious themes, well drawn characters, and realistic dialogue are now the rule rather than the exception."

Today's early teenager is pushed by the environment into a precocious adulthood. Children today have to grow up faster than we did. It shows in the books written for them.

For little kids, middle-age kids, and big kids—particularly the latter, the young adults—there is a "new realism." It started with Paul Zindel's honest, grubby, unsentimental *My Darling, My Hamburger* in 1969. As early as 1965 there was *Harriet the Spy*, in which the girl narrator records in a diary her wry observations of and about her parents.

Such realism is now standard in books for young readers, including mysteries. Juvenile books now deal with racial and ethnic situations, poverty, drugs, dating, teenage pregnancy, teenage marriage, child abuse, parental divorce, and death. Children today live in a tough society and a dangerous world. Even murder can be a subject for YA mysteries. Murder, rape, psychosis, and even international terrorism as it disrupts private lives can be written about for the young adult reader. Formerly, the only allowable sin for villains was greed.

The gap between juvenile mysteries and adult mysteries has been much reduced since the late 1960s, but there are still significant differences. Contemporary juvenile mysteries usually do not depict physical violence or torture in detail. There may be explicit sexual emotions and action but not for the sake of titillation. No hard men as heroes; no glamorizing of a hard-boiled detective. A very few sophisticated YA mysteries have young anti-heroes as protagonists, but these are not popular.

For young readers there are always a few characters to look up to, respect, and like. There is no absolutely bleak view of people, no bitter, completely despairing evaluation of life.

The big change is the new honesty and frankness. All the unpretty subjects mentioned above may occur in juvenile books to some degree, provided that they are truly an organic part of the story and grow out of the characters' motivations.

Some of the best examples of what we're talking about are in the YA novels of Jay Bennett: *The Long Black Coat, Dangling Witness, Deathman Do Not Follow Me, Pigeon,* and *The Birthday Murder.* Twice an Edgar winner for the best YA mystery, Bennett makes a point of being in direct contact with his readers. He travels around the United States, talking to and with young people in schools. His books have a depth which reflects the young readers' own depth of feeling and concern. In his Edgar-winning mystery, a fourteen-year-old boy idolizes his older brother who, after army service, has disappeared and may be dead. All the boy has left is his brother's long black overcoat. When the boy finally unravels the mystery of his brother's whereabouts and discovers that he was unworthy of such worship—well, this is a contemporary mystery. Many of Bennett's teenage novels are reprinted for adult readers as well.

Bennett writes:

The heart of the matter in writing for Young Adults is to be at all times completely honest. Contrary to report upon report . . .Johnny can read and Johnny can evaluate and Johnny has a mind of his own. And the same thing holds for Joan. These young adults care about being opened up to life. They want your work honestly to reflect reality. Time and again I've been brought up short by a letter or a questioner in the audience asking why my central character made this choice and not another which squared more with reality. On one level is the pure story (or mystery) and then underneath that are all the other levels of human behavior and philosophy. I try to get in as many levels as I possibly can and I find that my readers of all ages respond. Some intuitively and others quite expressively and concretely.

Phyllis A. Whitney points out the importance of "a strong personal problem weaving in and around the mystery, and carrying some current message for the readers—without preaching."

A blithe yet serious teenage mystery novel is Susan Dodson's *The Creep*, in paperback and optioned for the movies. It is remarkable for its solid subject matter as well as its insight into the agonies and joys of growing up. Ms. Dodson worked with the police department in her home city, Pittsburgh, to catch a rapist who preyed on young people. The nervy young heroine of *The Creep*, a volunteer trained by the police, acts as bait to lure the rapist out of hiding. She does this out of concern for their neighbor and baby-sitter, a girl even younger than herself whom the "creep" tricked and raped.

Ms. Dodson says that her mystery is based on two actual cases: the child rapist in her own area and the case of a child killer in Ann Arbor, Michigan, who was caught. Yet her book shines with humor and love and Americana. It affirms the courage and ability of good people to catch and stop the bad guys.

Dealing with another aspect of the same theme is Richard Peck's *Are You in the House Alone?*, which won an Edgar for the best juvenile mystery of 1976.

Other fine chilling examples, with emphasis on a boy's courage, are *Catch a Killer* by George A. Woods, (a rural setting you'll never forget), which was a Scroll Award winner in 1972, and *Deathwatch* by Robb White (an American desert setting you'll never forget), which won an Edgar in 1972. Don't forget Lois Duncan's brave girl in *Ransom*.

Joan Lowery Nixon, another two-time Edgar winner, observes: "The writing in a Young Adult novel is as involved as the writing in a novel for adults. The main difference is that the main character in a YA is usually a teenager." Seventeen is usually the protagonist's top age.

Dorothy Francis, well known for adult and juvenile mysteries, stresses character and motivations: "The 'why' behind a character's actions as he tries to meet a challenge or solve a problem is usually more important then the 'how' he uses in resolving his troubles"—troubles in which the mystery is an intrinsic part.

Realism pervades the dialogue in most YA mysteries. Set in contemporary America, they have a laconic, vernacular humor which rings true.

Does so much realism sound grim? There is quite another style of mystery novels for young readers.

History and legend in the American South and a very real and mystifying ghost illuminate the poetically written *The House of Dies Drear* by Virginia Hamilton, an Edgar winner in 1968. Timeless, too, are Joan Aiken's fantasy-mysteries, exquisitely written for older teens. (She is the daughter of the poet Conrad Aiken.) *The Stolen Lake* (1981) is the third in "a series set in the reign of King James III, supposing that he had been king of England in the 19th century instead of Queen Victoria."

This imaginary history along with that of King Arthur (adapted) and a wildly changed geography may not be for everyone, with its touch of satire and wry characterizations, but some of us cherish these fantasy-mysteries. Joan Aiken's powerful, bitterly realistic mystery of a few years ago, *Died on a Rainy Sunday*, has been reissued for young readers and adults.

For sheer delight and fun, read Kin Platt's *Mystery of the Witch Who Wouldn't*, which won an MWA Scroll, and his earlier Edgar winner *Sinbad and Me*.

The occult interests many young readers, who don't believe it can be explained rationally. *The Girl in the Grove*, a Scroll winner by David Severn, is a haunting and unforgettable mystery tale.

Mystery writer Stephen Mooser's *Into the Unknown: Nine Astounding Stories* is listed in Children's Choices for 1981 by the Children's Book Council as a "fascinating collection of mysterious events that defy explanation (a young girl's ability to see through walls, the sighting of a flying saucer, a man's disappearance into thin air). [It] appeals to even the most reluctant reader. A challenge to think critically about possible explanations."

In Madeleine L'Engle's *A Ring of Endless Light*, Vicky, sixteen, uses her telepathic powers to communicate with dolphins.

A 1981 anthology edited by Helen Hoke, *Mysterious, Menacing, and*

Macabre, includes "nine spine-chillers by Ray Bradbury, Roald Dahl, and other masters."

At the opposite pole from the occult are the rational logic puzzles, such as George Edward Stanley's mini-mysteries for readers eight to twelve. His brief, tightly organized mystery short stories, based on painstaking research, appear in such juvenile magazines as *Jack and Jill* and *Child Life*. Reading these stories is a game, a challenge, and an exercise in reasoning. The author is a full professor at Cameron University, Lawton, Oklahoma, where he teaches French, German, linguistics and semantics, and creative writing. Twelve of his stories are reprinted in a collection.

The Gothic mystery novel, that spooky and romantic descendant of *The Castle of Otranto*, is written for and widely read by teenage girls and a certain number of boys, too. *A House Full of Echoes* by Mara Kay deeply involves two young girl friends and the sophisticated older brother of one of them. He comes to visit at the baronial house now run by its impoverished owners as a girls' boarding school. Why does the empty ballroom blaze with light night after night? Why is an old tragedy being reenacted by these three young people?

Romances, contemporary as well as Gothic, embody intricately plotted mysteries in YA novels. Betty Cavanna's *Stamp Twice for Murder* maintains this author's consistently high standard. *The Horseman's Word* by Georgess McHargue combines mystery, romance, and horses. Literate and sensitive, *The Marina Mystery* by Constance Leonard involves sailboats and some flesh-and-blood young people. This is only the 1981 crop.

International terrorism is powerfully handled in *Detour to Danger* by Eva-Lis Wuorio, which is set in England and Spain. Its picturesqueness serves to underline the horror with which a sixteen-year-old Spanish duke (he's half Scottish) discovers neo-Nazis in his own house in present-day Spain. They are using the vast Moorish cellar of Nando's family villa as their meeting hall, complete with iron swastikas and a portrait of Hitler. Then Nando, furious, unafraid but wily, finds out that they have an assassin in their hire.

Sports provides crucial backgrounds for mysteries for boys and many girl readers. *The Horns of Danger* by Mabel-Esther Allen, for readers eight to twelve, is a rousing football yarn. *Hoops* by Walter Dean Myers takes us into contemporary Harlem, where a black basketball star of seventeen is befriended by a former pro who, the youth discovers, is mixed up in a point-shaving scandal. For boys of ten or twelve and well into their teens, *The Hoard of the Himalayas* by Larry Healey takes the reader into a memorable mountain climb and a chilling adventure.

It is striking that every range of subject appears in mystery and suspense novels for young readers in every age group. Some are highly individual and hard to categorize.

Hub by Robert Herring is a suspense novel of Americana that adults, too, can enjoy. Part folk tale, part legend, it is a realistic story of two boys in the backwoods, stumbling into unsuspected danger.

Interestingly, the Bible house of Moody Press publishes a mystery for early teens, set in a religious mission. It has plenty of action, violence, and genuine feeling. *They Called Him Shifta* by Dick Bohrer gives a firsthand picture of Americans in Ethiopia.

Margaret Goff Clark's *Who Stole Kathy?* is out of the ordinary in its feeling for a handicapped youngster. A deaf girl is kidnaped, and two of her teenage friends, with much danger and suspense, try to find and rescue her.

MWA's Edgar Award winner for the best juvenile mystery for 1981 is also a first-rate novel for YAs. A paperback, *Taking Terri Mueller*, by Norma Fox Mazer explores the dilemma of happy, breezy Terri, in her early teens. She lives in one town after another with her delightful father, an itinerant carpenter; her mother died years ago. Terri, wondering why they never stay put, finds out that her parents divorced years before and that her father kidnaped her. How Terri discovers that her mother is alive, locates her, writes to her with misgivings, joins her, and comes to know and love her—yet continues to love her father—constitutes a moving and fetching mystery novel.

Mrs. Mazer writes: "I read that there are an estimated 25,000 children stolen each year in the aftermath of divorce, and that most of them will never see their mothers again. I was not only saddened by this bleak statistic, I was also startled and fascinated that in the name of love, adults would deprive their children not only of a parent but of family and friends, community and stability . . . I wrote this book for both adults and children . . . to say, as in all my writing for children, 'Okay, life isn't easy but don't despair. There is strength inside you.'"

The classic mystery is always well represented. There is now an abundance of Sherlock Holmes spin-offs, from juvenile spoofs in which kids play at being the great Holmes in all too real and dangerous situations to adaptations of several of the original Sherlock Holmes stories for young readers.

Gimmicks can be fun. One house publishes juvenile mysteries whose last chapter is sealed but whose cover picture gives at least one main clue.

Who Killed Harlow Thrombey by Edward Packard, a Choose Your Own Adventure for readers eight to twelve, challenges the reader to act as detective by giving alternative chapter endings and a list of questions. If the reader chooses one course toward solving the mystery, he or she turns to one page; if another course, to a different page.

For reluctant readers with low reading skills, there are the special Hi-Los, "high in interest, low in reading skills." Norma Ainsworth's fine YA mystery novels are so persuasively written and have so much to say that the reader never suspects that *The Mystery of the Crying Child* and *The Ghost at Peaceful End* are Hi-Los. *Crying Child* is used as a model text of a children's mystery, Hi-Lo or not, at the Institute of Children's Literature in Redding Ridge, Connecticut, where Ms. Ainsworth is a consultant and an instructor in the graduate school. It is illustrated with photographs.

Another kind of mystery for reluctant readers is Sid Fleischman's "Bloodhound Gang Mysteries," with many new titles including *The Case of the Flying Clock* and *The Case of the Secret Message*. These are primarily action, and many have been seen in television versions.

Juvenile mysteries generate spin-offs: juvenile games, coloring and activity books, toy books, TV series, cartoons, and VCR tapes.

The young are naturally futurists, at ease with computers, excited about space exploration, and fascinated by electronic games. Small wonder, then, that science fiction now overlaps with suspense in novels for readers eight to twelve and for YAs.

Jane Yolen's *The Robot and Rebecca and the Missing Owser*, for readers eight to twelve, is set in the year 2121 and is an eye-opener. The girl detective has a robot for her assistant. *Walkie-Talkie Caper* by John Shearer features a small boy "Super Private Eye," complete with electronic equipment.

English juvenile suspense novels reprinted in the United States are particularly well researched and beautifully written. A small steady stream of fine novels from England in the late 1970s and early 1980s includes *Children of the Stones* by Jeremy Burnham and Trevor Ray. It recounts, with a sound knowledge of space-time physics, how a British astrophysicist and his young son, studying the magnetic properties of prehistoric stones in a village older than Stonehenge, find that the stones are aligned to a black hole in outer space. Father and son are caught in a time trap, "another continuum, a present in which the future can only repeat the past." The way back to the present is closed unless they can, at risk of their lives and as people die around them, solve an ancient mystery of symbols and rituals. They are forced to figure out and foretell accurately the movements of the planets in relation to these stones. Passages about the supernatural and the legendary can be read with naive literalness; they can also be read as mankind emerging from savages through advancing stages into our present civilization.

Instruments of Darkness by T. Ernesto Bethancourt has suspense, sci-fi, and occult elements—and a huge readership as a result. Of his earlier book, *The Mortal Instruments, Publishers Weekly* said, "A sophisticated, superbly crafted science fiction thriller . . . mature teenagers *and* discriminating adults will be mesmerized, baffled and chilled."

Children's Book Review Service loves it: "A rich combination of detective thriller and supernatural tale, this fast-paced novel for Young Adults offers much for thought [for] any reader who has ever given any thought to the questions of ESP, telepathy, or occult science in general."

The Homeward Bounders by Diane Wynne Jones, English and published in the United States in 1981, is part fantasy, part suspense as its young adventurers travel through other worlds. It has a solid basis of space-time theories and recent discoveries in space.

American authors, too, are writing space-age suspense for young readers, such as *Barney in Space* by Margaret Goff Clark, for ages eight to twelve, one of her well-liked Barney mysteries. Although his friends try to help him, Barney is transported to outer space and faces an enemy alien. The story is possibly more suspense than mystery, but young readers are too spellbound to worry about that distinction.

Nearly the same theme appears in a book for readers twelve to sixteen. *There Was This Man Running* by N. L. Ray, an Australian woman, is another mystery based on mental telepathy, this time with elements of science fiction. A dangerous alien from another world abducts Cass's sister, and he moves into a different time and space to search for her.

Are these books mysteries? They are suspense, certainly. They

are not the tightly plotted, step-by-step, deductive crime stories the
word "mystery" has usually connoted. They have a new approach,
expanding the field of mystery and suspense in a world expanding in
technological knowledge and into space.

This reader, for one, finds such books cogent, brilliant speculation
as well as a rich and rewarding reading experience. One remembers
that from the submarines of *Twenty Thousand Leagues Under the Sea* to
recent cartoonists, writers' fantasies and forecasts have come true. In
the nineteenth century, Jules Verne accurately predicted not only submarines but space travel. One contemporary sci-fi writer (Robert Hein-
lein? Isaac Asimov?) foresaw the use of heavy water in the manufacture
of the atomic bomb and described its construction while it was actually
being built. That author nearly got into trouble with the government
for his foresight.

Who is to say, in some of the current suspense/sci-fi fiction for
young readers, that there is not a prophet? The young have open minds;
they are the ones who will be traveling into space as technologies develop.

One extraordinary work of YA suspense literature is *The Awakening
Water* by G. R. Kesteven (English, 1977; reprinted in the United States,
1979). Whether labeled fantasy, science fiction, or a parable, it stands
out for its meanings and its excellent writing.

"After the devastation of 1997, thirteen-year-old Watford Nine
John accidentally breaks out of the regimen imposed by the Party and
decides not to return—" because the boy, thirsty while working with
his sluggish companions in the fields, drinks from the river instead of
drinking the drugged water given at their barracks. How he finds and
joins other young runaways who live off the land and how they evade
the dangerous authorities and fight back creates suspense that provides
a great deal to think about.

However, not all young readers are futurists. Children's literature
has always clung to traditional forms and life visions. Even in a techno-
TV world, there is continued interest in the past and in the imaginative,
in historical fiction and fantasy which "the techno-TV culture appears
inclined to reject," (Encyclopedia Britannica: "Children's Literature").

Exotic backgrounds and faraway times and places enrich several
well-written, well-researched mysteries every year, including 1981. Some

of these YA novels are based on the author's family history or background. One award-winning book, *The Village of the Vampire Cat* by Lensey Namioka, set in medieval Japan, deals with a village terrorized by a mysterious killer. The author is Chinese-American, and her husband is Japanese-American; this story incorporates some of his family history. *The Mystery of the Plumed Serpent* by Barbara Brenner brings Mexico alive for the reader. *Manwolf* by Gloria Skurzynski is set in medieval Poland. Although the mystery is slight, its setting and history are memorable.

There is solid reading and fine writing for teenagers, especially girls, in *The Whispered Horse* by Lynn Hall and *The Third Eye* by the Scottish author Mollie Hunter. Her novel exemplifies what she says in her critical volume *Talent Is Not Enough*: The writer for young people must have values and a viewpoint of his or her own.

Phyllis A. Whitney, whose adult and juvenile suspense novels are enduring, worldwide bestsellers, says much the same thing. Although she always puts entertainment first, Ms. Whitney writes: "In my books I've dealt not only with everyday human problems. I've written about racial prejudice. I've given young people a picture of Hiroshima as it is today. I've written about apartheid in South Africa. Not to bog down a story . . . never to preach. But to give substance and meaning and value, so that the book can't be dismissed as 'just another mystery.' And, of course, to satisfy my own need to write about precepts I believe in. Sometimes they are world-shaking problems, sometimes not—but they always are of importance to me."

Timeless and timely, Whitney's mystery novels for readers eight to twelve and for older teens include *Mystery of the Haunted Pool*, an Edgar winner; *Mystery of the Hidden Hand*, an Edgar winner; and *Mystery of the Scowling Boy* and *The Secret of the Missing Footprint*, both Scroll Awards winners.

Are sales up or down for juvenile mysteries? How do mysteries sell in comparison to other kinds of juvenile books? Asking questions at children's bookstores and at general bookstores in New York City elicited the answers.

Mysteries for young readers always sell very well. Series sell more than individual titles. The mystery series for readers eight to twelve sell especially well. At Doubleday bookstores the Alfred Hitchcock paperback series about three boy investigators "fly out of the store." *Encyclopedia Brown* is a consistent bestseller. The Choose Your Own Adventure series is a favorite.

Paperback juvenile mysteries sell more than hardcover. Libraries are the big purchaser of individual titles and of hardcovers.

Do juvenile mysteries sell better than other categories of juvenile books? No clear-cut answer emerged. "It's hard to compare," booksellers replied, and they cited excellent sales year in and year out for the C. S. Lewis Narnia fantasies and for Madeleine L'Engle's *A Wrinkle in Time* and Tolkien's *Lord of The Rings*. Salinger's *The Catcher in the Rye* is much read by YAs. Young adults buy Agatha Christie and other adult mystery novels along with YA mysteries.

Publishers Weekly, in its issue devoted to children's books for fall, 1981, notes that juvenile mysteries always sell. Even in years when book sales in general are down, mysteries retain their level of sales.

"Paperback mysteries for very young readers, or illustrated hardcover in inexpensive format, are widely displayed in racks at supermarkets, neighborhood newspaper shops, airports and bus terminals. They are frankly entertainment and are bought like cookies or coke," says *PW*. "Bookstores devoted exclusively to children's and YA books always have a sizeable mystery collection."

General bookstores reported steady juvenile mystery sales. And there are book clubs for juvenile mystery buffs where they, or their parents, can subscribe and buy by mail.

PW reports recent changes in the market: "Traditionally, schools and libraries have been the main customers of the 2500 to 3000 children's titles issued annually. Recently, however, sales in bookstores directly to the public have been increasing, despite higher cover prices. Bookstores used to sell 20 to 30% to the public. One editor told PW, 'We expect that 60% of our books will be to the general buyer in the near future. . . .' With the proposed deep slashes in federal funding, this is encouraging. . . ."

PW calls children's bookstores "a labor of love (requiring) an in-depth knowledge of children's literature and an unending stamina." About two-thirds of the stores note that fifty percent or more of their titles are in paperback editions. Some of the children's bookstores reported that most of the books were bought by parents or other adults who ask the bookseller for advice on what to buy. Children know what they want to buy or they ask other kids. Fiction sells best, especially series.

The quality of mystery fiction for children varies greatly. Some series books have been criticized. They are defended on the grounds that they "hook" a youngster into reading and open the way for books of more substance later on.

Quality or not, series characters have become part of the American life-style for young readers and adults. Once when I was alone in a strange town, the day's business finished and an empty hour until plane time, I was comforted and pleased to find my old friends Archie and Edith Bunker on the hotel TV set.

What influence do juvenile mysteries have on young readers? On young lives? First and obviously, the books which are more than entertainment, the books with the most to say, make the deepest impact on impressionable young readers. A character the young reader admires and sympathizes with provides a role model. The obverse is true, too. Read about a weak or obnoxious character, and you'll try to avoid his traits in yourself. Although indirectly implied, the author's viewpoint and ethical values can and do influence young readers.

Career information is painlessly, often engagingly imparted at a time of life when some young people are beginning to think of choosing a future occupation. To see, via a book, exactly what a space engineer does and what place he earns in society can be useful. Many women of all ages have told me that they became nurses because they had read my Cherry Ames nurse mysteries.

The picture of various cultures, of various classes and ethnic groups, sheds light for the young reader. It helps him understand his own community, become aware of his place in it, choose what place he wants in it, and choose how he may want to change and improve the community. Many young readers say they've found truer, deeper portrayals of people and society in books than in movies and on television.

Finally, there is the reassurance—"I'm not alone, I'm not the only one stuck with this problem"—whether it be acne, social awkwardness, or the tension of having divorced parents or new half brothers and half sisters. Or just not being the smartest kid in class or the top star on the basketball team. Or facing of the finality of death, the death of someone you love. Constructive answers are suggested indirectly in some juvenile books.

What does the future of the juvenile mystery hold? That's like asking what the future of our society and our world holds. We can only guess that mysteries for young readers will always deal with universal personal themes and change as times change; but they will always fascinate.

TWO

On Technique

6

The Spy as Hero and Villain
Ken Follett

Is it possible for a character to be both hero and villain? The answer is yes; this is part of the process of creating character and building suspense. How is suspense created? I do it in three steps, and the first—perhaps surprisingly—is to create characters. I used to think plot was more important than character, and that's one reason I wrote many unsuccessful novels. A cliff-hanger, for example, is not suspenseful unless you care about the man who is hanging there.

> Jones hung by his fingers from the edge of the cliff, shuddering with fear. He looked down to the beach fifty feet below. The tide was out.

This is a little dull because we don't know who Jones is. But try this:

> Jones hung by his fingers from the edge of the cliff, shuddering with fear. He looked down to the beach fifty feet below. Peter saw him and shouted: "How did you get up there, Dad?"

Simply by making Jones somebody's father, we have begun to create suspense. Everybody has parents, and most people have children, but in many thrillers the hero is a loner who comes from nowhere: a man with no past, perhaps even an orphan, probably a bachelor or divorced, usually childless. It is thus more plausible that he should jet around the world at the drop of a hat, seduce beautiful women, and risk his life on the turn of a card. Nobody's father would risk his life

74

on the turn of a card. But as it so often happens in fiction, it pays to take the difficult way out, to find a plausible reason why somebody's dad should risk his life that way. Think how much mileage John Le Carré gets out of Smiley's unfaithful, desirable, and always distant wife. Of course this kind of thing can also be cheap, as in *The Fifth Horseman* (1980), in which the detective has a handicapped child. (However, subtlety should not be overrated. That book sold millions, which means a lot of people liked it.)

So, in creating character, I like to start with the person's parents. Suppose we want to write a story about a campaigning journalist. Newspapermen in fiction are often drunk, coarse, and shabby, prepared to lie, cheat, and betray their friends for the sake of a story. We will avoid cliché. Let us speculate about the parents of this journalist, who might as well be called Jones.

They must have been verbal people who talked to each other intelligently and told their children bedtime stories. They probably read books and newspapers and had interesting dinner guests.

Since Jones is a *campaigning* journalist, he must have got his idealism from somewhere. It might be a direct inheritance. Perhaps his father was a civil-liberties lawyer. It might be indirect. The parents might have been devout Catholics so that the child, though an unbeliever, feels the need to be devout about something. Or it might simply be that his mother was a deeply compassionate woman—this would be my choice.

A campaigning journalist is probably antiestablishment. He must have good rational reasons for his beliefs, but he also has emotional reasons. At some time in his life, I would say, he has felt part of a minority within society, so I would make his parents refugees, or cranky vegetarians, or Jehovah's Witnesses, or Communists. Let's make them Communists.

He sounds like an overachiever, so he will be the eldest child, but we'll give him a younger sister to help him get on well with women in later life.

So, a Communist father, a compassionate mother, a lively intelligent family, and a kid sister. We haven't got his character yet, but we know where he's coming from. Now let's jump thirty years.

Jones is married with two children and works for the *New York Times*. How does he get on with his family? He often stays late at the office, and he travels a lot; thus, we might expect him to neglect them, but I would do the opposite.

I should say a little more about this business of doing the unexpected. It is as important in fiction as in music. Let us forget Jones for a moment and consider writing a novel about life in a Siberian prison camp. We know two important facts about such camps: They are awful, and people stay there forever. The temptation is to concentrate on the awfulness and the length of time by writing a harrowing ten-year saga. It takes a storyteller to emphasize the passage of time by writing a novel spanning only one day. And it takes a genius to write about a good day. The novel I have in mind is *One Day in the Life of Ivan Denisovitch* (1963). If Solzhenitsyn had written about a bad day, the book would be merely gruesome; but the smallness of Ivan's triumphs and his disproportionate elation at the end of the day break your heart.

We can't write as well as the masters, but we can steal their tricks. Thus, our journalist will be a good father, a light drinker, and an upright and principled man. His father's somewhat academic idealism is tempered by his mother's warmth, and thanks to that sister, he likes his wife and she likes him. Jones is beginning to emerge as a rather attractive fellow. We should give him some faults.

I had the reverse problem with Henry Faber (*"die Nadel"*) in *Eye of the Needle*. He was a convincing villain who needed some likable traits. He had to be a ruthlessly efficient killer in order to survive as a German spy in wartime England; but then, in the second half of the book, he had to be so attractive that a beautiful and decent English housewife would fall in love with him.

The answer is spelled out in Chapter 21:

He switched on the little lamp beside the bed. The effort tired him, and he slumped back on to the pillow. It frightened him to be this weak. Those who believe that might is right must always be mighty, and Faber was sufficiently self-aware to know the implications of his own ethics. Fear was never far from the surface of his emotions; perhaps that was why he had survived so long. He was chronically incapable of feeling safe. He understood, in that vague way in which we understand the most fundamental things about ourselves, that his very insecurity was the reason he chose the profession of spy: it was the only way of life which could permit him instantly to kill anyone who posed him the slightest threat. The fear of being weak was part of the syndrome that included his obsessive independence, his insecurity, and his contempt for his military superiors.

In other words, there are two layers to Faber's personality. On the surface he is tough; underneath he is vulnerable.

It's always good fun to peel away layers of character during the course of a novel. Indeed, there are professors of English literature who believe that this is what novels are *really* about. One of the attractions of writing about spies is that they always have at least two layers, since they live lives of deceit; and one of the attractions of reading about spies is that a spy's public image is an extreme case of the kind of false front we all put on from time to time.

Furthermore, Faber's duality parallels a conflict in the emotions of many of my women readers, who are both drawn to and repelled by dangerous men. The reader of *Sweet Savage* historical romances has solved this problem by marrying a bank clerk and devouring tales of girls who get raped by pirates. Lucy's affair in *Eye of the Needle*, in which she makes love to a dangerous man and then kills him, is the same fantasy with a feminist twist.

Faber's dual character is revealed in the first chapter of *Eye of the Needle*. We learn that his landlady finds him attractive; then he kills her; then he throws up. The landlady's feelings tell us he's a good guy; the murder tells us he's a bad guy; and the throwing up tells us that the good guy is disgusted by the bad guy. If I were writing the book again, I would try to display Faber's personality more gradually and subtly.

However, the reader gets a chance to forget the nice guy underneath during the next forty thousand words as Faber murders a whole bunch of generally nice, harmless people. Then he is washed up, half dead, on Lucy's doorstep.

Until this moment he has been invincible because, living in the solitary world of furnished rooms in London, he has been anonymous. People don't know who he is until he sticks a knife in them, by which time it is too late. On Storm Island it is impossible for him to conceal his true self because his vulnerability has become physical; he is forced to live cheek by jowl with David, Lucy, and Jo; and most importantly, he finds himself irresistibly drawn to Lucy's warmth, beauty, and passion. The conflict between what he *does* and what he *is* can no longer be suppressed. Such conflicts are difficult to write about, and the perceptive reader will have noticed that I dodged the task by concentrating on Lucy in the second half of the book. If I'd had the courage to confront Faber's dilemma, I might have written a better book. But perhaps we should move on to step two.

Having gotten the reader interested in a convincing character, we must proceed to get the reader worried about him. Jones must meet with the greatest crisis of his life. He will probably discover some information so explosive that Certain People are prepared to kill him to prevent his spilling the beans. This is a routine kind of crisis (in fiction, anyway), and readers will not yet be impressed. Think: Jones wouldn't risk his life for the sake of a newspaper story; he cares more about his family than about the *New York Times*. Who wouldn't? Now we see why thriller heroes rarely have families.

But let's take the difficult way out and keep the family. Suppose this is the biggest story of Jones's life. Furthermore, his career, though once promising, has recently suffered a nasty setback. (Perhaps he wrongly identified an Argentinian janitor as Martin Bormann, all over the front page.) Suppose his wife, more decisive than he, urges him to run the story, saying she will never respect him again if he suppresses it.

Now let us complicate matters. Jones has a mistress. The mistress gave him the story. For some reason, there is no way he can run the story without revealing to the world (and to Mrs. Jones) that he has a mistress. Furthermore, when these facts are explained to the mistress, she insists that he must not run the story. Now Jones has an emotional crisis on top of a career crisis, and we're getting somewhere.

The crisis is not quite bad enough yet. The story must have a personal importance for Jones not only because it's a good story but also because of what the story is about. If the story is about medical malpractice, Jones must have had a child who died at birth because of bad doctors. If the story is about dope peddlers, Jones's kid sister might be a junkie.

And the story must be of public importance so that millions of people would suffer if Jones were to sit on it. Both these requirements might be met as follows: Jones's father died in jail, having been convicted of spying for Russia. Jones has learned that the principal witness against his father was in the pay of the Mafia. And that witness is now the United States Attorney General.

Now, I think, we have the reader not just interested but worried: about Mrs. Jones, about the mistress, about the kids, and about Jones's career, personal honor, and integrity. What next?

In *The Key to Rebecca* (1980), Vandam's crisis develops like this. First he learns that a German spy has slipped into Cairo. This is not so much a crisis as a routine work problem. Then he finds out that the spy is getting first-class information and sending it to Rommel. This makes the routine problem a crisis. By this time Vandam is falling in love with the girl he's using to trap the spy. This makes the crisis personal. Then the spy gets hold of the Allied plans for what could be the decisive battle of the desert war. This makes the crisis public. Finally the spy escapes Vandam's trap, taking with him not just the plans but also the girl and Vandam's ten-year-old son, thus creating the biggest crisis of Vandam's life.

The reader who pauses to reflect at this point will realize that the kidnaping of the boy is hopelessly implausible. The spy, who up to now has been very smart, has nothing to gain and a lot to lose by taking the child. I tried to get over this problem by having the spy go a little crazy toward the end, but of course that is cheating, and finally I settled for making sure that the reader did not pause to reflect at the crucial juncture.

Step three is structuring the story, the hardest thing to explain because so much of this process is instinctive.

At the start of the book, the danger will be relatively slight and rather distant. The tale will unfold in an ascending series of climaxes, each more agonizing than the last. At first Jones will see the crisis only in terms of his career. Then his father's reputation will be thrown into the balance, to be followed by his sense of duty, his love for his mistress, and his personal safety. Toward the end he will realize his wife and children are in physical danger. When the suspense is unbearable, we will tighten the screws even more. The reader, who began by being interested and then became worried, will soon be absolutely terrified.

All this is easier said than done, but I have run out of explanatory formulas. All I have left is a few notes and observations on story structure.

Note that we have four main characters. Jones, Mrs. Jones, the mistress, and the attorney general. The reader must like Mrs. Jones and love the mistress (or vice versa) in order to believe that Jones feels the same. The attorney general could be simply a monster—sometimes it's nice for the reader to have someone to hate—but my preference would be to make him a fully rounded human being with plausible reasons for the villainous things he does. Again, the difficult way is best.

The story must develop because of the choices made by the main characters. Jones must not be a mere victim of events. No doubt, the Mafia will sooner or later shoot at him. In our story they will do so as a result of something he or his wife or his mistress has done. That shot will not come out of the blue. Every major decision made by one of the characters must affect some or all of the others. We must not develop the story by wheeling on a long-lost cousin, an informant, a Mafia hit-man, or a cop.

"Credibility" is the key word. Our story—in case you haven't noticed—is rather farfetched. After all, an attorney general in the pay of the Mafia? So everything our characters do, even when they make mistakes, must seem to them and to the reader to be the most sensible thing to do in the situation as it then appears.

The big crises must last a long time. When, finally, Mrs. Jones learns about the mistress—as she must, for in general all the secrets must be revealed—the scene should be a long one. Her finding out is something that Jones, and the reader, have been worried about for many pages; when it comes, the reader wants to live it. Similarly, when Jones has a fistfight with the attorney general—a likely way for two such enemies to finish up in a thriller—the fight should go on for several pages. My own technique for such fights is to forbid myself to finish the scene before it is six pages long. This is crude, but it's better than short fights.

The fight between Jones and the attorney general will probably be the biggest scene in the book, and so it should come right at the end, when the reader knows everything that is at stake, the enmity between the two men is fully developed, and each of the characters is desperate. In general, it is a terrible mistake to have the most dramatic moments come halfway through the book, for then the rest of the story is an anticlimax, which happens, in my opinion, in *Kane and Abel* (1980), otherwise a rather good piece of storytelling.

Well, we've ended up with a story about a moral dilemma, but this should not surprise us. Moral dilemmas have been the stuff of fiction since long before the novel was invented (let alone the thriller)—think of Hamlet.

Having made the reader successively interested, worried, and terrified, we must leave him satisfied. The best ending I've ever written is in *The Man from St. Petersburg* (1982), and I'm not going to spoil the story by giving it away. Suffice it to say that the ending does not have to be happy, but it must resolve all the major problems raised in the narrative, not just the central problem of physical danger but also the emotional, personal, and career problems of all the main characters and the related political or military problems. When the reader puts down the book, he must feel as if he just got off a roller coaster. It was fun, it was scary, he's relieved it ended okay, and one day soon he's going to take another ride.

7

The Education of a Mystery Writer

D. R. Bensen

First as editor and lately as writer, I have spent much of my professional lifetime dealing in one way or another with what is in publishing called genre fiction and often, by those outside the trade, hackwork: mysteries, Westerns, science fiction, Gothics, and romances (even, for a while, the short-lived category of nurse novels). I came into publishing amply furnished with the prejudices of an English major, an assumption that authors were people like Homer, Cervantes, Shakespeare, Dostoievsky, Hemingway, and Eliot, and that the rest were at best contributors to what Dr. Johnson called "the publick stock of harmless entertainment." All the same, I cherished a private relish for the entertainers, including the so-called hacks.

That's not at all strange, actually. For me, the fun of reading came long before any critical assessment of what was being read, and a good, fast story with colorful characters and a plot that wasn't too hard to follow had it all over literary quality. I took in the junk and the good with equal avidity and relished the Bobbsey Twins as much as *Treasure Island* (more, in fact—about the first editorial judgment I ever made was that first-person narration is harder to follow than third) and Tom Swift (bless Mr. Damon's buttons) as much as Alice.

Later, I saw nothing odd in switching from Shaw or Shakespeare to Phoebe Atwood Taylor or Maxwell Grant and then back to Homer or Auden. (In some cases, the switch could be accomplished with a single author, such as turning from the poetry of C. Day Lewis to the detective stories of "Nicholas Blake.") Later still, in college, the lines were drawn more rigidly between authors and others, with the others being regarded as unworthy of attention or emulation. As with other juvenile practices, what had been an innocent activity took on an air of sinfulness and was therefore pursued with greater interest and stealth. Instructors and professors of those days would scarcely have approved the growth of "contemporary studies" of the work of popular writers, especially in the fields of mystery and science fiction.

I did begin to see, though, that much of what I enjoyed in the trivia I read by choice was present in the acknowledged classics: action, bloodshed, and bawdry. Even the most lurid pulp magazines would have hesitated to try out on the audience some of the riper bits of Rabelais or to present Odysseus as a role model. *Crime and Punishment* was a great psychological study but also a crackerjack crime story, with Porfiry Petrovich as implacable a detective as Holmes or Nero Wolfe. It began to dawn on me that even authors wrote in part because they enjoyed telling lively stories. As Don Marquis's cockroach Archy put it, commenting on literary excuses for Shakespeare's coarser passages:

> he pulled rough stuff
> and he liked rough stuff

At the turn of the half century, I discovered that the possession of a bachelor's degree in the liberal arts was no qualification for gainful employment, and so I entered publishing. (Readers familiar with the conditions of the trade will see no contradiction here.) One of my first tasks was to draw up a chart of sales of paperback books by category for the years 1950 and 1945. As 1950 was not much more than half over and publishers did not make their sales figures public, a good deal of approximation was involved. (My collaborator, now editor in chief of a major paperback house, and I burned our notes as soon as the job was done to avoid awkward questions about methodology.) But I think that in the main the conclusions were correct. These were that in the first ten years of the paperback industry in this country (Pocket Books began it late in 1939) the top-selling category by far was mysteries, with Westerns second and classics and major modern fiction and non-fiction well down the list.

It seemed, then, that I had found my way into an industry where a taste for and an understanding of Agatha Christie or Mickey Spillane (category reading makes for strange bookshelf fellows) was of more use than the ability to spot the next Jane Austen. At least the skill had market value, and apparently I could get paid for what I had been doing for amusement. I found that working with this sort of writing increased my enjoyment of it and gave me a new respect for it. As a reader, I had known only that some mysteries and science-fiction stories pleased me and others didn't. As an editor, I now had to understand why they pleased me or not and guess whether they would please enough people to make my various employers enough money so that they would be willing to go on being my employers.

Making these judgments for reprints of books already published was not all that daunting. After all, somebody presumably more knowledgeable than I had already decided that they were worth doing in the first place, and so I couldn't go far wrong in recommending them. (This was a fallacy of inexperience, as anybody who has known editors can testify.) However, after a few years, I was afloat in the full tide of original paperback publishing, and that was another matter—dealing with manuscripts. After all, one sheaf of typescript looks much like another, and there is precious little advance winnowing of what comes across an editor's desk. The day's offerings may include some top-notch material, are almost certain to include material far more abysmal than an innocent public would believe, and will probably have something that might be modestly successful with further work.

It was when I got to this point that I began to learn something of my craft and how it bore on my private enthusiasms. I had to learn what it was that made a good story and a publishable book and how something that just missed the mark could be altered so as to score a bull's-eye. That, of course, led to working with writers. (I earlier said that I used to distinguish between authors, the serious kind who get into school syllabuses, and others, the "ordinary" writers; but I learned fairly early that in publishing usage an author is nothing but a writer who has a contract.)

Most of these writers were of the sort described as hacks, men and women who turned out books steadily, making much or all of their living at that work and able to take an editor's suggestions for alterations in their stride or produce one or another sort of book on assignment. I dealt enough with some of the more exalted crowd to confirm what I had come to feel in college: there was not that much difference between the two groups. One writer might be trying to work out a knotty moral, philosophical, and artistic question in a narrative that tested writer, editor, and reader to the utmost. Another writer might be concerned with how to get a barbarian warrior through a maze of monsters and wizards. But both, to the extent that they were professionals, were working with the same tools and facing similar problems. And both—again, to the extent to which they were professionals—would take intelligent, concerned suggestions for the solutions to these problems and (though often with frightful yells and lamentations) use at least a few of them, sometimes actually to the improvement of the work. (I think most writers—and authors—cherish the notion of having two editions of at least one of their books published, one with and one without editorial input, believing that the latter model would do far better in reviews and sales. My experience as an editor suggests that they might be right; my experience as a writer, that they're probably wrong.)

Manuscript editing is a peculiar process. There is no real training for it or any but the loosest standards, such as not removing a seemingly superfluous character and then finding out that in the writer's view he was the lead. It is rather as if a surgeon, presented with an anesthetized patient, were to have to decide, on the basis of experience, intuition, and personal taste, how that patient ought to be rearranged to best advantage. In the hands of a really vigorous practitioner, the patient may well come out from under the ether with an unexpected new nose or a sex change. A few shaming experiences of this sort, combined with a natural indolence, led me to the course I followed through most of my editorial career: figure out what the story's strengths and weaknesses are and then tell the author and let him or her do the work.

One great value of this method is that the editor is constantly learning from authors, who, especially in the years of the editor's apprenticeship, usually have a lot more experience. I remember Will Jenkins, whose first science-fiction story appeared in 1917, giving me a remarkably useful insight on scene setting. "That chapter I set in Paris, now," he said. "Did you get a sense of the place, the color and so on?" I agreed that I had. "Well, go back and read it, and you'll find that there's almost *no* detail in it—I just said that they were in Paris, at a sidewalk café, and let the characters play the scene. You supplied the rest from everything else you've read about Paris."

The immediate benefit of this tip was to allow me to cut lots of scenic descriptions from manuscripts I was working on, to their considerable benefit. Recalling it has allowed me, as a writer, to avoid overloading my editors and readers with detail they don't need or want.

I also learned from the very bad—the inept, the unpublishable work—that came across my desk. The faults of a competent or more than competent craftsman can be subtle and hard to discern at first reading, but those of the really awful ones spring to the eye. After a while it became possible for me to see that what Joe Pro had done in a certain section of his manuscript that made me feel uneasy was a smoother version of the howler that Charlie Clunk had perpetrated in his unreadable opus. (I don't, by the way, entertain an attitude of total derision for the Charlie Clunks. Given persistence, energy, and willingness to learn, they can improve, and I know of at least two who have gone from Clunk status to respected publication.)

After a while, then, I could without gulping or blushing suggest to a veteran whose work I had been reading when I was twelve that the manuscript he had just turned in would profit by having the first third redone entirely and dropping the parallel drawn between sexual intercourse and the current economic situation. I wasn't quite confident enough to say, as one editor is reported to have done, "Listen, Vladimir, it'd work better if it was a little boy that Humbert goes ape over instead of a girl—trust me," but I was pretty free with my suggestions and got on the whole a cooperative reception.

By this time, the term "hack" had almost disappeared from my professional and personal vocabularies. I was working with writers who could do the job and—rather more briefly and unhappily—with writers who couldn't, and that was the main concern. I could turn from working on a series Western to a sensitive and important study of the ecology with no sense of incongruity or abashment and come up with suggestions that each writer could take and at least profess gratitude for.

I had, it seemed, learned a lot about editing. Then, following one of the killer typhoons—accompanied by volcanic eruptions, earthquakes, plagues, famines, and cascades of fire and brimstone—that periodically afflict the publishing trade, I found that I was no longer an editor, at least not an employed one.

Very well, then. I should in a quarter century have learned something about writing from one side; I might as well use that knowledge and write rather than edit. I had, as I have said, deleted "hack" from my lexicon, but now it came back to my mind strongly. I had no ambitions to make a major statement on any matters of transcendental importance or any conviction that I could kindle in myself the kind of fire that allowed people like Robert Ludlum and Harold Robbins to blaze away at the top of the bestseller lists. Cold water cooks no potatoes, and the utility bills have to be paid if the pot is to boil, and so potboilers were the immediate need.

Aside from the incidents and insights I have mentioned, I had a few guides. One came from the autobiography of John Masters, author of *Nightrunners of Bengal* and other bestsellers. He told of having been turfed out of the Indian Army at the end of World War II, along with all the other British officers, and being faced with the prospect of making a living outside the military. After an unsuccessful try at selling a patent brassiere in the United States, he figured that the life of a writer, if it could bring in the cash, would suit him. He then proceeded to compose a novel as if he were doing an intelligence report, keeping in mind the facts, the intended audience, and the impression he proposed to make. The Book-of-the-Month Club took it.

During my last term on a payroll, I had the privilege and pleasure of working with Leonore Fleischer, who at that time was the acknowledged expert in turning screenplays into readable novels for paperback publishers. She once advised me: "If you're writing something and you can't think of anything to put down that isn't lousy—dull, a cliché, or whatever—put it down anyhow. Just don't stop. You can always go back and correct it—and, about half the time, you'll find that it reads okay, a lot better than you thought it was when you wrote it."

At this unnerving juncture, I also recalled something I had heard on a BBC interview with Alistair MacLean. The plummy-voiced host had asked the author of *The Guns of Navarone* what he read by choice. MacLean answered, in broad Scots accents: "When Ah want to read a guid story . . . Ah write one."

The first assignment I got after I had gone beyond the editorial pale to that wasteland where writers dwell was to write four Gothic novels, deriving their plots from the astrological signs of the heroines. Masters's dictum came into immediate play. I consulted standard astrological manuals and was able to draw up parallel lists of characters and their quirks, preferences in colors, perfumes, lucky days and numbers, and so on. Once I had done that, the plot began to emerge almost on its own. It was a frightful effort to write them, but it was a fantastic feeling to get to the end of one book and realize that the fact that the two villains' signs were earth and water called for them to be, for the best of plot reasons, stuck in a patch of mud at the climax. Until then I had never realized that the reason people write is that it is, at certain moments, about the most fun you can have with your clothes on.

All the same, the whole business smacked of hackery. Then, when the convergences of interest of an agent and a publisher brought me to create and write what is called an "adult Western" series, there was rather more of a reek than a smack. Is it possible to run off a bunch of books with an irresponsible lead character with a taste for casual sexual encounters and frequent incidents of violence and not let down the whole concept of intelligent entertainment? Looked at one way, no. On the other hand, going into the background needed to make the books plausible, I learned a lot. (Even at the lowest level, some kind of plausibility is important. John Creasey in his younger years, with imperfect information, essayed Westerns and came up with a memorable description of his hero riding across the plains at sunset, "while, from far above, came the mournful cry of the circling coyotes.") I know a good bit more now about how things were on the Western frontier between 1870 and 1880 than I ever learned in school.

I found myself trying to construct the tightest plots I could, being economical with settings (thank you, Will Jenkins), forcing my way through the morasses of establishing motives and characters no matter how horribly banal they seemed to be as I slammed them out on the typewriter keys (thank you, Leonore Fleischer), and trying to come up with a story I would enjoy reading once it was written (thank you, Alistair MacLean).

By some kind of accident I can't recall, I put the Lone Ranger into one of these books—not identified as such, but with plenty of clues— and have since employed Scarlett O'Hara, the Wizard of Oz (who vanished from the Midwest in a runaway balloon in the late 1870s on his way to the Emerald City), and Sherlock Holmes as subsidiary characters. Having seen a lot of this private kind of fun in manuscripts I was expected to publish, I had learned that you can't do it unless the story would work for readers who didn't know the references. Some will guess that my Mrs. Butler of 1879, a hard-nosed businesswoman operating in Texas, is actually Scarlett O'Hara fourteen years after, but the story has to hold up without that knowledge.

So here I am, with twenty-five years of category publishing behind me and five years of writing the stuff also behind me and that indeterminate period between now and the time it will make financial sense for me to recline onto the pillow of Social Security ahead of me. Have I turned into a hack?

I am a little old to worry about that, but I have had twinges in my leg or shoulder, like Dr. Watson and his jezail bullet. But no longer. Last fall I fell into conversation with one of the most professional writers I know. I gave him a horror story about slow payment from a company I was doing work for; he gave me a worse one. He had been asked to put in a proposal for a paperback series, and, as always, had given it his best shot. The proposal was rejected. "You know, Pro"—as I shall call him to protect the justifiably bugged— "you write too well for the clowns we publish for."

Well, there it is at last, the essence of hackery. A writer may not feel all that great about putting out a saga of range warfare or the curious doings of slime molds in a distant galaxy, but if he's a pro, he'll do it as well as he can; if it works, he'll have a reason for satisfaction. He can rightfully consider himself a craftsman, no matter what kind of implausible, lurid, or foolish premises he's working from.

But if a writer—or an editor, bank president, or plumber—ever truly despises what he or she is doing and the people he or she is doing it for, that plumber, bank president, editor, or writer deserves the name of hack in its worst sense.

8

If the Book Is So Good, Why Isn't It in Hardcover?

Franklin Bandy

What is the genesis of a suspense novel that wins an Edgar Award for the year's best paperback original? To put the question again, if the book is so good, why wasn't it published in hardcover?

As an aside, it would be helpful if people would stop referring to these books as paperbacks. Think of the author's feelings. "Paperback" sounds so flimsy and cheap. Actually the cover is heavy card stock and feels like plastic, and the title is sometimes embossed. The more considerate term is "softcover." Nice people say "a softcover original." Remember, even if they are flimsy, they are rapidly becoming not cheap.

I would like to say that the Edgar-winning book went directly to a softcover publisher because I could make more money that way. A writer frequently receives a modest advance from a hardcover publisher and then must split the much larger softcover advance fifty-fifty with the hardcover publisher. If the writer goes directly to paperback, he or she gets the whole thing. It could have happened this way. I have had several books published in hardcover and then split softcover reprint money with the original publisher.

However, it must be admitted that my agent did not first submit *Deceit and Deadly Lies* (1978; originally titled *The Black Box of Kevin MacInnes*) to a paperback publisher. This manuscript was read by the wrong editor in a number of hardcover houses. I'm only half joking. I think many editors are as subjective in their judgments as nonprofessional readers.

If a manuscript grabs them, they'll fight for it. There are numerous editors in the big hardcover houses, and I'm sure the right one would have loved *Deceit and Deadly Lies*.

Basking in its success as a paperback original, I taunted one of these negative editors (who happened to be a personal friend) with her poor judgment in turning it down, what with its spectacular sales and winning an Edgar, etc.

She smiled at me brightly and said, "Well, as we all say, sh— sells (expletive partially deleted).

One problem with *Deceit and Deadly Lies* was that it was something different. In fact, it was something completely new in a four hundred-page suspense novel format. First, it was weak in danger. The protagonist was in mortal danger only about twenty-five percent of the time instead of the required ninety-nine percent. (I strive too hard for credibility, though I am not always successful.) Second, it had a somewhat tangled love story, sexy but not just sex with a voluptuous enemy agent who is going to try to kill the protagonist immediately afterward. (The spider lady syndrome is practically a necessity.) Third, the protagonist had an unusual specialty. He wasn't a worn-out, shabby ace agent; he wasn't a good-guy hit-man, or an amoral hit-man, or even a goody-two-shoes who draws the line at anything worse than maiming an enemy for life. His specialty was finding out the truth.

How did I become involved with this truth seeker? It all started with a small article in the *New York Times* describing a new invention that provided a more flexible and more accurate method for detecting lies than the polygraph. The polygraph monitors four bodily reactions to stress: blood pressure, pulse, respiration, and galvanic skin response. In order to provide all these reactions, the subject must be wired up more than a rock group. An accordion tube must be strapped across the chest to measure respiration, a cuff goes on the arm to measure blood pressure and pulse, and wires are attached to the hands to measure galvanic skin response. Trussed up in this way, the subject is plain scared to lie.

The new instrument, the PSE, or Psychological Stress Evaluator, required only a tape recording of the voice. Feed this tape through the PSE, and it electronically measures stress through the muscle micro-tremors of the voice. It seems that your voice may sound perfectly natural when you're telling a lie or making some other stress-producing statement, but these tiny muscle microtremors can give you away when examined by an instrument sensitive enough to measure them. I thought this was a bit hard to understand until I found that the wristwatch I wear has a quartz chip that vibrates thirty-five thousand times to measure one second. If they can measure that, they can measure anything.

At the time I was working on a mystery novel which was later published under the title *The Bold House Murders* and was looking for something to give it a special cachet, something new to add to the complex solution. With this in mind, I telephoned the company that manufactured this space-age marvel, Dektor Counterintelligence and Security, Inc., at that time located in Springfield, Virginia (near Washington, of course). After explaining my problem to Allan D. Bell, Jr., president and coinventor of the PSE, he said, "Come on down and we'll give you a demonstration."

Beth, my wife, and I drove to Springfield and had a meeting with Allan Bell and C. R. McQuiston, coinventors of the PSE and both formerly lieutenant colonels in Army Intelligence. I had met other agents working in international intelligence, but these two seemed tougher and sharper. As a worn-out, lovably human ace agent, I would not wish to tangle with them.

The afternoon was given over to a long briefing on the workings of the PSE; then McQuiston demonstrated by testing me with it. I answered about half of his questions with lies, some deliberate and others because there are questions you can't answer quickly and simply with the truth. For instance: "What's your favorite color?" I said, "Blue." Actually there are shades of blue I like and shades I detest. Score one inadvertent lie. The machine was impressively accurate, catching me in all my deliberate lies and pointing a finger at my confused answers.

So I used the PSE in *The Bold House Murders*. This was a mistake. Even though the PSE was only peripheral to the solution of the crimes, one reviewer carped about the murders being solved by a phony lie detector machine. Newgate Callendar didn't review it at all in the *New York Times*, a blow because he had reviewed the other two books in this series. Even the most ardent admirer of the series, Richard Watts, writing in the *New York Post*, said: "Franklin's *The Bold House Murders* at first seemed to me the least interesting of his novels about a hypochondriac detective and his ex-hippie assistant. . . . Then he somehow whisks his plot to the North Pole and it suddenly becomes very fine. . . ."

This review didn't help, even though the North Pole portion was worth more than the price of the book. The research alone was worth the price of the book: old *National Geographics* all over the place, telephone calls to the North Pole (well, to a place practically at the North Pole), numerous visits to the Canadian tourist information office, and so on. Did you know that the average citizen can get there? You, who never dreamed of being an arctic explorer, can stand right on the same North Pole with the greatest. But bring money. If you want the details, you'll have to read *The Bold House Murders*.

The blatantly unfair reception of *The Bold House Murders* discouraged me. I said, "No PSE will ever again darken the pages of a novel of mine."

Fortunately, this prejudice softened with time. We received an invitation to attend a symposium at Dektor devoted to the use of the PSE. This meeting was to be attended by about fifty psychologists/psychiatrists and law enforcement people from around the country, who would discuss the results obtained with the PSE. We were particularly intrigued by the use of the PSE in psychiatry, and it appeared to be an interesting way to spend a weekend.

The meeting had dramatic moments. One hard-nosed New England psychiatrist described a setup in which he had the PSE hooked up to a tape recorder hooked up to his telephone, all on his bedside table. When a patient called him in the wee hours, he could run the conversation right through the PSE while talking and act accordingly. In one instance a patient called at 3 A.M. and told him that unless he saw her immediately, she was going to commit suicide. Glancing at the PSE graph chart winding out, he said, "See me at nine o'clock in my office without fail. Good night," and hung up.

All the other psychologists/psychiatrists in the room began to jump up and down yelling, "No! No! You can't do that!"

"Yes I can! And I will!" yelled back the sturdy PSE enthusiast.

For a moment we thought there might be a lynching, but after a while things quieted down.

Another topic the mind probers explored was the problem of hypnosis. Does the subject really tell the truth under hypnosis? Some claim that hypnosis is no truth drug. The subjects, they say, tend to give answers they think the hypnotist wants them to give. Others say no, the truth will out.

In an attempt to resolve this matter, tapes of subjects being questioned under hypnosis were put through the PSE. I could be wrong, but I don't think a definitive conclusion was obtained.

I asked Beth whether she remembered.

"No, I remember only about the woman who wouldn't stop answering questions," she said.

I, too, remembered the incident.

One woman under hypnosis kept answering questions long after the hypnotist had stopped asking. Question after question that had never been asked was answered. Efforts to bring her out of the trance failed. More questions were answered.

Finally, in desperation, the hypnotist bent over her and said, "Excuse me, but I believe you have had a small personal accident. Now don't let it concern you. It does happen once in a blue moon."

Answers ceased. The woman gave him a glassy look of horror and scurried off to the bathroom.

Beth said, "Actually, what he said to her was, 'Excuse me, but I believe you have your pants full.'"

"I can't write that," I yelled.

"Well, whatever. That's what he said."

So much for the psyche experts. But comedy aside, a number of these professionals mentioned that they found the PSE useful in revealing areas of stress in a patient's recollections that the patient was not aware of, having buried the traumatic aspect too deeply in the subconscious.

The law enforcement people were polled on the efficiency of the PSE as compared to the polygraph. With one exception they all reported excellent results. One felt that the polygraph was slightly more accurate but admitted that the ease and flexibility of using the PSE was a big plus.

We returned to New York favorably impressed. The PSE was undoubtedly here to stay, but it was questionable whether it had any further significance to me as a writer. It offered a way out that was much too easy. Its use in solving a protagonist's problems was on a par with having the U.S. Marines arrive at the last minute.

At this point, I had not really grasped the complex problems of stress analysis, whether provided by the PSE or by the polygraph. Both were magic gadgets that gave you peaks and valleys of lines on a graph chart. You looked at the chart and said, "Ah ha, see, right there he told a big lie." Such is not the case. Both instruments measure only stress, and stress can be caused by various human reactions: anger, fear, nervousness, embarrassment, deception, guilt complex reaction, etc.

For instance, there are people who react with guilt to crimes they have never committed. A good examiner may throw in a question such as, "Did you take Mrs. Smith's diamond ring?" when there is no Mrs. Smith and she has not had a diamond ring stolen. If the subject's answer "no" is loaded with deception stress, the examiner knows that he has a lulu on his hands.

In short, neither of these instruments is magical. The magic lies in the area of the examiner's knowledge and skill. It involves not only the ability to ask the right questions but the possession of a computer-type mind that can scan the very subtly different stress markings, weigh a few hundred or a thousand possibilities, and then zero in on the correct interpretation. Sometimes the pattern makes the solution easy; at other times it is more difficult to unravel than the *London Times* crossword puzzle. On occasion, results must be marked "inconclusive" because even the best examiner cannot decipher the clues with certainty.

In 1974 the writer George O'Toole bought a PSE and used it in a wide-ranging and thorough investigation of the John F. Kennedy assassination. This great tragedy was then eleven years old, but in its day it had been the media event of all time. Everyone connected with it had been interviewed on television or radio or tape recorded. There were eyewitnesses, police, members of the Warren Commission, medical examiners, and many others involved directly with the investigation. These tapes were available, and many of those participating were, of course, still alive. O'Toole not only traveled around the country interviewing as many of these people as possible and taping these conversations, he also spent days feeding dusty tapes from television station, radio, library, and other archives through the PSE. Assisting him in analyzing these tapes was C. R. McQuiston, my old friend from *The Bold House Murders*. I was again on the way to becoming hooked on the PSE.

O'Toole's book *The Assassination Tapes* was published in 1975 with considerable fanfare. Gigantic posters decorating the sides of New York City buses were only a small part of the advertising and publicity blitz. The book was a sensation because O'Toole had in his interviews found many contradictions, evasions, and apparent outright lies producing hard deception stress. A portion of the public was already convinced that the Warren Commission had inadvertently or deliberately engaged in a cover-up of the real truth of the assassination and the events leading to it. The conspiracy aspect was fortified by Jack Ruby's background. It was difficult for many to swallow his explanation that he killed Oswald because he was so upset about Jackie and JFK's children. Thus, the O'Toole book reopened the can of worms. It provided a multitude of questions that needed answering; it provided evidence that could keep investigators working for another fifty years.

I was then completely unaware of McQuiston's association with O'Toole's project. At the time of the hullabaloo, I had a gloomy little office in an apartment in New York City's Upper East Side (we live about twenty-five miles from the city) and was working away, when I got a telephone call from McQuiston. He and O'Toole had that morning appeared on the *Today Show*, and he, McQuiston, wanted to talk to me. I suggested that he come over.

The apartment was on the second floor and had high windows overlooking the blacktop roof of an adjoining one-story building. I'm a little hazy on what happened, but it seems to me that McQuiston came in through the window. At least the first image that comes to mind is of him looming over me, standing on the windowsill. He said it was because I didn't answer the buzzer. A likely story. He was probably on the roof casing the joint in case I might be having a conference with the KGB and need terminating with prejudice. Figuring out where apartment 2-J was would have been no problem.

Anyway, he jumped gracefully from the sill and grabbed a chair, and we began to talk. His proposal was that we work together to produce a big book based on his experiences.

Impressed with the fascinating information in the O'Toole book and the celebrity status of everything surrounding the PSE, I agreed to put aside a novel I had half finished and take another fling at the PSE.

Since McQuiston had to do a lot of traveling from his base in

Florida, solving big cases similar to those dramatized in *Deceit and Deadly Lies*, our working together required careful planning. We set a tentative date to meet for a weekend in one of the big hotels near the Philadelphia airport. There we would spend hours taping a lot of talk.

On the date agreed upon, a fine Saturday morning, Beth and I set out for Philadelphia. Philadelphia is a relatively easy city to find, but this chain hotel, allegedly visible from the highway, somehow evaded us. You may notice that I'm not mentioning the name of the hotel. Subsequent events which I am about to describe made me feel that it would be kinder to let this hostel remain anonymous and also make me less liable to become a party to a lawsuit. Anyway, we did finally find this hotel, which one could see from the highway, but it was another branch located fairly close to Harrisburg. Setting our compass, we backtracked to Philadelphia and eventually located the right establishment, several hours late.

McQuiston, whose busy schedule makes him a bit edgy, had been telephoning everywhere. However, he took our delay good-naturedly, and after a late lunch we retired to his room to set up our tape recorders. Beth retired to our room to sleep, feeling that her presence might inhibit our discussion.

We had hardly started our work when the hotel registration clerk called to tell me that my credit card was no good; he requested that I report to the front desk immediately and explain myself.

This particular card had a credit limit of about $3,000, with payments made promptly every month, and less than $100 outstanding against the credit limit. They were making me look like an improvident bankruptee or credit card cheat to a man with whom I was about to enter into a financial partnership.

I went fuming and muttering down to the desk. Stolid resistance. I was guilty until proved innocent. The clerk telephoned in the number again and received the same answer.

"I'll sue," I said.

"Not us; you got to sue Citibank," said the clerk.

I had a vision of me and Citibank's lawyers squaring off in court. David and Goliath. What a majestic spectacle! On the other hand, David had had quite a buildup with the citizenry, but who would know if I ducked the issue?

I said, "Don't you worry, I'll take care of them."

Fortunately, I had ample cash with me, which is not always the case. McQuiston, who had accompanied me down to the desk, had a hearty laugh to brighten his day.

To skip briefly to Monday, the first call I made was to the credit card complaint department. I found them less than sympathetic.

"It was a mistake," said the representative. "Everybody makes mistakes once in a while. That's why they put erasers on pencils."

"I can see that I'm going to have to call Dave Rockefeller," I said.

"That would be nice," she said. "Mr. David Rockefeller is a lovely person, and since he's chairman of Chase Manhattan, well—"

What a blunder! "I know that, but I'm sure he's a friend of, ah, what's your chairman's name again?"

"That's for me to know and you to find out," she said.

I asked, "Look, how would you like to sleep out in the rain some night because the hotel wouldn't honor your credit card?"

That got to her. She wept for a while, and we parted friends.

But to get back to Philadelphia, we returned to McQuiston's room and taped a good three hours of discussion. Each of these cassettes has background music. In the room across the hall there was a little dog with a high-pitched yelp and tremendous stamina. He didn't miss a beat in three hours.

McQuiston, who carries more than one tape recorder, put an extra one by the door to record the dog. After dinner, he took this recorder to the desk and turned it on with the volume as loud as it would go so that the clerk and everybody in the lobby and/or restaurant could enjoy the concert.

The clerk said, "I'm sorry, sir, we'll move you to another room immediately."

McQuiston said, "You, sir, will move the dog to another room."

"Ur, yes sir, ur, the dog. We'll move the dog. Right!"

McQuiston, who sometimes projects an aura of menace, said, "Immediately."

"Ur, immediately, Yes, sir."

This was the clerk who had been so snooty to me about the credit card. How sweet it was to see him groveling!

We went back to McQuiston's room to tape until midnight. We decided that the story would center on a superexpert undone by his own genius and arrogance. He's the world's best PSE examiner. His talents and knowledge have made him very rich, a multimillionaire like McQuiston, though modesty would force him to settle for being one of the best. MacInnes, the protagonist of *Deceit and Deadly Lies*, is *the* best. This professional expertise gives him power, and in using this power, he begins to play God with it. In two cases his arrogance becomes his undoing, with the second one undermining his professional reputation, since it causes the suicide of a prisoner accused of murder who is later proved innocent.

I said, "At this point he will go steadily downhill until he loses all his money, becomes virtually a bum. Redemption will finally turn him around, assisted by the love of his beautiful mistress, Vanessa, and he will fight his way back to the top."

"Never," said McQuiston. "He will not lose all his money. That I won't stand for."

"But why not? He's got to take a disastrous fall."

"Not his money. He won't lose all his money."

We argued awhile. It was as though I was trying to take McQuiston's own expensive car away from him. Finally I understood. A writer can take all the hero's millions away from him in chapter 10 and see that he gets them back in chapter 20. Hard-boiled realists like McQuiston hate to see this even in fiction. They know it's damned near impossible to get all those millions back.

I asked, "Well, how about this? He becomes an alcoholic." I added hastily, "Only temporarily, of course."

McQuiston grudgingly agreed.

We knocked off for the night, and I went back my room. I had hardly gotten into the room, when McQuiston was outside, pounding on the door.

"There's a fire! Get out of the building!" he yelled.

I turned to my sleeping spouse. "Beth! Fire! Get a robe and let's go!"

Beth is not a fast dresser. Of course, she was half asleep. I think she was back in the Reubens Hotel in London, dressing to go across the street to the Queen's garden party. Actually, the Reubens is across the street from Buckingham Palace's royal stables, but they're pretty interesting, too. A lot of the "county" squires who come to London to attend the Queen's garden parties stay there. We once shared a connecting bath with a bishop of the Church of England, a nice old gentleman who occasionally became disoriented and wandered into our room.

McQuiston and I spent five minutes jumping up and down and yelling out in the hall until Beth finally appeared. By the time we got to the lobby, the fire was out. Some drapes on our floor had been set on fire.

We then learned that the employees of the hotel were on strike.

It was a bit odd, sleeping in a hotel with the employees on strike, assuming that one of them had perhaps set some drapes on fire. But I don't remember it bothering me particularly. I was too tired.

Sunday we resumed taping and acquired another five hours of discussion. We also set up a modus operandi for future operations which would not require our meeting.

During the following months we mailed tapes back and forth; as soon as I had completed a chapter, I would mail a photocopy of the pages to McQuiston. He would vet them and mail them back suggestions. In the course of some nine months, the novel wound its way to completion.

Then came the difficult part: selling it. I turned the manuscript over to my literary agent, Oliver Swan, of Collier Associates. He liked it. Ollie is a gentleman of the old school and won't try to sell anything he doesn't like.

It was fortunate that he approved, because if he believes in something, he never gives up. As I mentioned earlier, there were numerous rejections by the hardcover houses. During this period, agents who had been in the business a long time, such as Oliver Swan, were not too keen on paperback originals. Paperback houses were companies that reprinted hardcover books. Although he still retained the manuscript, I think Ollie had just about given up on *The Black Box of Kevin MacInnes* (which would eventually become *Deceit and Deadly Lies*).

It is possible that the manuscript would still be gathering dust unpublished were it not for a bright young editor named Michael Seidman. Temporarily unemployed, he was beginning to feel the pinch. He was hungry. His little daughters, age one and three, were hungry. They were getting only one bowl of gruel a day.

One day they both held up their empty bowls and wailed, "More, Daddy, more."

The three-year-old was old enough to know better. "You ask for *more?*" Michael shouted. "I'll apprentice you to Angelo Findeltoppe Ghastly, the undertaker. You'll be adorable in black and white dimity, leading the processions for children's funerals. You cry nicely, without too much noise."

"Not *that*, Daddy, please. I apologize," said the three-year-old, but her eyes were big with resentment and hurt.

Michael was touched. He decided that he could no longer sit at home and wait for a call from Doubleday or Simon & Schuster. He would sally forth into the world of publishing sans safe editorial niche and weekly paycheck. He would become a packager on a small scale, perhaps later on a big scale.

He began contacting agents he had dealt with as an editor, searching for unrecognized gems. He called on publishers. His strongest tie was with Ace Books, the mass-market paperback affiliate of Grosset & Dunlap. He became a middleman, with his arrangement calling for him to get a percentage plus a nonreturnable advance in return for delivering a fully edited manuscript along with cover concepts and promotional ideas.

Oliver Swan had a manuscript that intrigued Michael. He hurried to Ace with *The Black Box of Kevin MacInnes*. It was read by the editorial director, who rejected it.

Michael slunk away. The bad months of 1977 continued to be bad.

In September, things began to fall into place for him. Ace had acquired the distribution rights to another paperback list and were starting a new imprint, aimed primarily at the male market. The list would go under the name of Charter, and the management at Ace wanted to know if Michael would be interested in coming in and heading it. He asked whether he could have three or four seconds to think it over.

As executive editor of Charter, Michael's first acquisition move was to offer *The Black Box*. The editorial director again turned it down.

Early in October, the editorial director resigned. Seidman immediately acquired the rights to *The Black Box*.

The first problem he had to confront, now that the book was his, was the title. *The Black Box of Kevin MacInnes* was not a selling title. Working in concert with Tom Doherty, then president of Ace Books, Pat Crain, Charter's associate editor, and Susanne Jaffe, Ace's editor-in-chief, Michael came up with a selection of possible titles. This list sorted itself down to two, *The Lie King* and *Deceit and Deadly Lies*. Shorter is better when it comes to titles, but the second title almost had the ring of romance, then the hottest-selling genre. So *Deceit* it was.

Now the process began. How to package the book? Seidman's problem was not knowing what was possible at a new, relatively small house. His experience at Fawcett and NAL led him to believe that it might be best to do the book as a "second lead," which means that while it would get some support, it would not get the kind of commitment that might make a difference. The book's position on the list has a lot to do with what goes on the cover and how much is spent producing that cover.

It was at this time that Tom Doherty, president of Ace, decided to see just what his new editor was doing. He read *Deceit* and sent for Michael. Michael experienced what is occasionally referred to as fear and trembling. The book had been turned down twice. Was he about to play a return engagement with unemployment?

Doherty was enthusiastic about *Deceit*. The outcome of the meeting was that my book was made the lead title for November 1978. As a lead title, of course, more could be spent on producing the book and on promoting it. It was decided to go with the title big, giving the illustration second place, an approach often used to give cachet to a book. In order to make the title jump, it was decided to emboss the words. Then as now, the extra expense this represents (whether it is embossing, foiling, stamping, or another trick of the trade) gives the wholesalers, retailers, and the ultimate buyer the sense that the book is important, that it is something they should know about.

A promotional piece, a flier, came next, along with a press kit, all of which spoke as much about the PSE as they did about the book. When it was announced that Sadat's speech to the Israeli Knesset had been taped and analyzed by the PSE, Charter felt that they were home free.

Bound galleys, celebration lunches, and a really great review in *Publishers Weekly* followed. Michael Seidman grabbed the first copies of the book off the presses and sent them to the awards committee of the Mystery Writers of America. The year before a book Michael had edited at NAL had been a nominee; this time he was certain Charter was going to have a winner.

April 1979 was a gala month for the Bandys. It was the first time we had ever attended the Edgar Awards dinner free, as guests of a publisher, and seated at the publisher's table. I had always envied writers who were thus honored. I hoped that *Deceit* would not let the publisher down and shame us all.

It was a great evening. The grand ballroom of the Biltmore Hotel had never been saturated with more friendly ambience, presenting a scene that shall forever be etched in full color in my memory.

Deceit and Deadly Lies was my first paperback original. Since then I have had three more novels published in this form. With the cutting back of fiction lists in the hardcover houses, the consensus is that more and more fiction writers will be turning to softcover originals. One hardcover house's current projection for the year is one hundred fifty titles, one hundred thirty of them nonfiction and twenty fiction. This is a bit extreme, but according to Michael Seidman the average hardcover publisher is moving close to seventy-five percent nonfiction and twenty-five percent fiction. Among softcover publishers the percentages are reversed, with nearly seventy-five percent of the list devoted to fiction. This trend has tended to further upgrade the quality of paperback originals, which in the dim past had largely been cheaply produced and cliché-ridden genre books for specialized markets.

There are two aspects of this switch from hardcover to paperback originals that I would not have anticipated. The foreign-rights sales of the paperbacks have been almost as good as those of my hardcover novels; in fact, *Deceit* was translated into Japanese. Although my hardcover novels received the attentions of one of the hottest agents in Hollywood, there was nary a nibble for any of them. By contrast, my paperback originals are doing nicely, without any help from the West Coast agency. Two are currently optioned, and another is in the hands of a well-known producer who is anxious to produce it and is at the moment working on the logistics. This is not the usual hearsay that filters back to the writer fourthhand via the producer's aides, the West Coast agency, and the New York agency. The producer has been corresponding directly with me.

The last question, I suppose, is, Will I ever go back to hardcover? Will hardcover ever come back to me? Who knows? Writers have very sensitive egos, and hardcover is still the prime ego trip.

9

*Mystery Movies: Behind the
Scenes*

Edward D. Hoch

I've learned a great deal about television and movie adaptations since
my first short story was dramatized on the old *Alfred Hitchcock Show*
back in 1965. My stories have been done well and done poorly, rendered
faithfully and twisted completely out of shape. Television and the movies are like that.

Perhaps the first mystery writer to suffer indignities at the hands
of the film adapters was Sir Arthur Conan Doyle, whose Sherlock
Holmes was portrayed in a short film as early as 1903, the same year
as that pioneering narrative film *The Great Train Robbery*. Movies in
those days generally ran ten minutes or less, and it's unfair to begin a
critical review of screen adaptations with such a preliminary period.

But by the following decade, at least one of the pet peeves of
mystery writers and readers alike had surfaced for the first time on
screen. The film version of a classic detective novel had omitted the
author's detective! A silent 1915 version of *The Moonstone* by Wilkie
Collins eliminated Sergeant Cuff. In the years that followed, this sort
of tampering with an author's creation was to become all too com-
monplace. To cite just two of many examples, the Sam Spade character
was called Ted Shayne in a 1936 version of Dashiell Hammett's *The
Maltese Falcon*, which we'll discuss later, and Ellery Queen is absent
from an otherwise reasonably faithful adaptation of Queen's *Ten Days'
Wonder*, released in 1972.

Happily, no one has yet attempted a film version of *The Hound of the Baskervilles* without Sherlock Holmes, but how is it that such classic detective characters as Sam Spade and Ellery Queen can be so easily omitted? The answer lies in the fact that the screen and the printed page are two different media. In adapting a published short story or novel for the screen, certain liberties must necessarily be taken. For one thing, the average mystery novel contains many more pages than the average feature-length film script.

In deciding what stays and what goes in an adaptation, the screen-writer must be granted a certain amount of leeway. The budget of the film, the director's needs, and even the star's wishes are factors to be considered. It's not surprising, therefore, that the standard contract for a film or television sale grants the producer the right to make any necessary changes in the author's creation. It's extremely rare for an author to have any control whatsoever over the final screen version of his or her book—even when that book has been a bestseller—unless the author has an actual financial interest in the production.

In fact, even the screenwriter loses control once the script of the adaptation leaves the typewriter. It may be altered or completely re-written by others, whole pages or scenes may be scrapped by the director during filming, and the final cut of the film—often dictated by the distributor—may not please the director. The original author, at the start of a long chain of creative decisions, is forgotten. (Cornell Woolrich was not even invited to the opening of the popular film version of *Rear Window*.)

But this brings us to another question. If the original author seems so expendable in the scheme of things, why is he or she necessary at all? Why purchase a property that is to be changed and rewritten, often to the point where it bears little or no resemblance to the original? Take the case of Dashiell Hammett's first novel, *Red Harvest* (1929). The book is a hard, tough private eye novel in which the nameless Continental Op cleans up a corrupt town after more than a score of murders. It was filmed by Paramount within a year after publication, but this 1930 movie version, *Roadhouse Nights*, was a comedy-melodrama with Charles Ruggles, Helen Morgan, and Jimmy Durante that bore no resemblance to the original source.

Obviously, a film company does not pay relatively large sums of money for a book it has no intention of using, but as was pointed out earlier, a great many things can change along the way. In this instance, perhaps it was the casting that played a large part in the direction taken by the final story line.

Hammett's second novel, *The Dain Curse* (1929), fared much better when it was finally filmed as a television mini-series in 1978. The poorest of the author's five novels and the only one not previously filmed, it had the advantage of nearly five hours of running time to help make sense out of a complicated plot line. Some critics thought this was far too long for the material, but at least the finished product was reasonably faithful to its source.

The mini-series, a relatively recent development during television's past decade, has provided an effective solution to the problem of translating the countless characters and events of a long novel to the screen. Especially in the hands of British producers, with their large pools of fine acting talent, adaptations of classic novels—both mystery and mainstream—were able to win both ratings and awards during the 1970s. From Collins's *The Moonstone* through the novels of Dorothy L. Sayers and up to John Le Carré's highly contemporary *Tinker, Tailor, Soldier, Spy*, the British mini-series did very well by the classic mystery.

But to return to the films of the pre-World War II years, it is with the three versions of Hammett's *The Maltese Falcon* that both the problems and the possibilities of screen adaptation can be most fully studied. After publication of the novel in book form during 1930, it quickly sold to Warner Brothers for a 1931 film starring Ricardo Cortez and Bebe Daniels. This first version of *The Maltese Falcon* was a reasonably straightforward rendition of the book, although it lacked any great distinction in directing or acting.

When Warner decided to remake the film five years later, they naturally needed a different title and certain superficial plot and character changes. The 1936 film was called *Satan Met a Lady* and starred Warren William as a more debonair detective named Ted Shayne. Bette Davis costarred in the role later made famous by Mary Astor. The falcon statue became a horn filled with jewels, and the menacing "fat man" became a hulking old woman.

This film version met with little more success than the first, and five years later Warner tried it once more. This time, with John Huston directing Humphrey Bogart and Mary Astor in the lead roles and with fine support from Sydney Greenstreet, Peter Lorre, and Elisha Cook, Jr., a film classic was born. A close comparison of Hammett's novel with the film or with Richard J. Anobile's book reconstruction by means of fourteen hundred frame blowups (*The Maltese Falcon*, Film Classics Library, Avon/Flare Books, 1974) shows how closely Huston followed the source both in the writing and the direction. (Huston wrote his own screenplay for the film.)

Compare, for example, the end of chapter 4 and chapter 5 in the book with the film scene in which Joel Cairo (Lorre) comes to Spade's office for the first time and pulls a gun on him twice. The dialogue and movements of the characters are almost identical, and even the contents of Cairo's pockets are exactly as described by Hammett. Again and again the film echoes the novel, down to the smallest detail. This is a faithfulness of adaptation rarely seen today, and it played no small part in the lasting fame of Huston's film. Even today *The Maltese Falcon* remains one of the best adaptations of a classic mystery novel to be put on the screen.

One minor change does come at the very end of the film. The police indicate to Spade that they have arrested Gutman—the "fat man"—and the others. In the book, they report that Gutman has been killed by Wilmer, the young hood he tried to double-cross.

Continuing with Dashiell Hammett's novels for the moment, we find two versions of *The Glass Key* (1935 and 1942) and, more significantly, the first of the Thin Man series. MGM's 1934 production of *The Thin Man* warrants our attention for a number of reasons. It is perhaps the best example of Hollywood's taking a detective character— or team, in this case—that appeared in a single book and creating a series from it.

As most mystery readers know, the title *The Thin Man* is not a reference to detective Nick Charles but to the murder victim, an inventor who is missing as the book and film open. The film proved such an instant success with the public that five more adventures of Nick and Nora followed: *After the Thin Man* (1936), *Another Thin Man* (1939), *Shadow of the Thin Man* (1941), *The Thin Man Goes Home* (1944), and finally *Son of the Thin Man* (1947). "The Thin Man" had come to mean Nick Charles in the public mind, even though actor William Powell was not particularly slim.

But more interesting for this study is the fact that the films continued on from the single original work. Hammett contributed the original story idea for the second film, and the third one was a reworking of one of his pulp tales about the Continental Op ("The Fare-well Murder"), but he took no part at all in the three films that followed. In this era of the 1930s and 1940s, when urban film palaces generally opened a new double bill each week, Hollywood produced far more movies than at present. At least half of them were so-called B pictures, running a little over an hour and generally having mystery or Western plots. Although the Thin Man series were all A films, playing at the top of the bill, most other mystery series of the period were second features. In an effort to fill this spot on the bill with a constant stream of new pictures, studios naturally turned to series, just as television was to do a decade later.

Nick and Nora Charles were not the only characters stretched far beyond their creator's single work. A lengthy Boston Blackie series grew from one book of connected short stories by an ex-convict, Jack Boyle. Some sixteen films about the Falcon originated in a single Michael Arlen short story, "Gay Falcon," in a 1940 issue of *Town & Country* magazine. And series about reformed crook Jimmy Valentine and Western outlaw the Cisco Kid each had their origins in a single short story by O. Henry. It's interesting to note that in all four of these cases the screen presentation of the character is softened from the hard-boiled original.

Not only was a character softened and made more likable for a series run, when circumstances demanded, he could even be killed off. The Falcon became the only American series detective ever to die on screen when actor George Sanders relinquished the role to his real-life brother Tom Conway in a film titled, appropriately enough, *The Falcon's Brother*.

It would be easy to say that the contortions suffered by mystery plots and characters in this period were the result of inept screenplays turned out by Hollywood hacks. But as we have seen, one of the best of them, *The Maltese Falcon*, was the work of John Huston. And many lesser films were often the work of well-known mystery writers. Stuart Palmer and Craig Rice wrote some of the Falcon screenplays, and Dash-iell Hammett and Raymond Chandler both worked in Hollywood on various projects.

Chandler's second novel, *Farewell, My Lovely* (1940), became in fact the basis for the third Falcon movie, *The Falcon Takes Over*, two years before the definitive screen version with Dick Powell as Philip

Marlowe in *Murder My Sweet* (1944). Chandler's third novel, *The High Window* (1942), was likewise used as the plot for a Michael Shayne movie, *Time to Kill*, five years before George Montgomery starred as Marlowe in *The Brasher Doubloon* (1947).

The Marlowe films made in the 1940s from Chandler's first four novels generally treated their source material well, allowing for the quirks of individual directors, such as the "subjective camera" technique of Robert Montgomery in *Lady in the Lake* (1946). Two later remakes in the 1970s starred Robert Mitchum as Marlowe. *Farewell, My Lovely* was carefully set in 1940s Los Angeles, but *The Big Sleep* transported Marlowe to modern England, where the story suffered in spite of liberal use of Chandler's dialogue.

Another writer of the period much favored by Hollywood was James M. Cain. His short novel *Double Indemnity* was successfully filmed in 1944 with a screenplay by director Billy Wilder and Raymond Chandler that brought them an Academy Award nomination. This was quickly followed by a filming of Cain's novel *Mildred Pierce* (1941), its drama enhanced for the screen by a climactic murder that does not appear in the book.

Cain's best-known novel, *The Postman Always Rings Twice* (1934), was filmed in 1946 and again in 1981. Although the later version was able to be much more explicit sexually, it unaccountably ended with the accidental death of Cora, completely eliminating the final chapter of the novel and the ironic point of the movie's title.

The mid-1940s also saw the first and best of three film versions of Agatha Christie's classic novel *And Then There Were None*. Although the ending of the film is quite different from the book's conclusion, there is a very good reason. The book was first published in England in 1939 with the unfortunate title *Ten Little Niggers*. It proved so popular that Christie quickly converted it to an equally popular play, but for the stage a new ending was needed. The book's finale, with everyone on the island found murdered and a later letter from the killer explaining everything including his own suicide, did not make for good stage drama. The play ended, instead, with the lovers left alive, facing the murderer and outwitting him. The film *And Then There Were None*, although it used the book title of the American edition, was really a film version of the play. This play, also called *Ten Little Niggers* in London, was titled *Ten Little Indians* in its American version, a title which served for the two later film versions and for some later American editions of the novel.

Different as they are, both versions of the ending are excellent. It's a rare example of one ending working best in print while another works best on stage and screen. The main difference among the three film versions of the book and play is in the setting. Originally set on an isolated island, as it is in the 1945 film, the action moves to a snow-bound castle in the Alps for the 1965 version and to a luxury hotel in the Iranian desert for the 1975 film.

The stage and film versions (1957) of Christie's excellent short story "Witness for the Prosecution" also differ from the printed version by continuing on for an extra page-and-a-half of dialogue and a dramatic final murder. The killer, who escapes punishment at the end of the short story, receives justice of a sort. Both versions work well, with the film version adding a final ironic bit of dialogue.

Recent years have seen extremely faithful screen versions of three more Christie novels: *Murder on the Orient Express*, *Death on the Nile*, and *The Mirror Crack'd*.

We have seen how some mystery plots suffered at the hands of film-makers, and perhaps this is the best place to treat the movies of Alfred Hitchcock, whose career spanned six decades and whose techniques often enhanced the books he chose to film.

One of the most famous spy novels of all time is John Buchan's *The Thirty-nine Steps* (1915), a portrait of pre-World War I espionage that became Hitchcock's first undoubted masterpiece when he updated and filmed it in 1935. Yet the ending of the movie, in which the cryptic meaning of the title is revealed in a theater during Mr. Memory's act, does not appear in the book at all. The steps of the title, originally stairs down a Kentish cliffside by which spies could escape to a waiting submarine, are transformed into the name of a secret spy organization. Hitchcock and his screenwriter, Charles Bennett, also added a love story to accommodate Robert Donat's costar, Madeleine Carroll. Despite the grumblings of British critics at such liberties, there can be little doubt that Buchan's fine novel was actually strengthened by Hitchcock's treatment. The plot is remembered today mainly in its popular film version, and first-time readers of the book are often surprised to find their favorite scenes missing.

Hitchcock's *The Lady Vanishes* (1938) was another that improved on the source material, a good but hardly outstanding novel by Ethel Lina White called *The Wheel Spins*. The fame of the movie caused the book to be retitled in most of its subsequent reprintings. But the director's habit of changing plot lines and altering endings was not always for the better. *Suspicion* (1941), which brought an Academy Award to actress Joan Fontaine, suffers from an ending which is a complete reversal of the book's conclusion. It must be said in Hitchcock's defense that he wanted to use the book's ending but was forced to bow to studio pressure. RKO was not about to let Cary Grant be portrayed as a wife murderer. (Some years earlier MGM did cast James Stewart as the killer in one of the Thin Man movies, but this was before his on-screen personality as a slow-speaking, honest hero had been firmly established.)

In 1951, Hitchcock took an excellent novel by Patricia Highsmith, *Strangers on a Train*, published the previous year, and transformed it into a masterpiece. By changing the protagonist's occupation from architect to tennis pro, the director was able to include a memorable suspense scene at a tennis match. True, the film ending is different from the book's and much more upbeat, but both versions satisfy.

Cornell Woolrich's fine novelette *Rear Window* became the basis for a 1954 Hitchcock film of the same title. Once again, love interest was added, this time in the person of Grace Kelly, and other characters like Thelma Ritter in the role of a visiting nurse helped to relieve the somewhat claustrophobic qualities of the original plot. But James Stewart as the protagonist confined to his room with a broken leg, who sees evidence of a murder through his rear window, is quite faithful to the spirit of the Woolrich original.

During the 1950s, the French mystery-writing team of Pierre Boileau and Thomas Narcejac produced two novels—*The Woman Who Was* (1954) and *The Living and the Dead* (1956)—which might have escaped notice in this country had it not been for a pair of remarkable screen adaptations. Both mysteries revolve around characters who may or may not be dead, and the film versions were eerie masterpieces of the director's art. The first became the classic 1954 French film *Dia-*

bolique, directed by Henri-Georges Clouzot, and the second became the 1958 Hitchcock film *Vertigo*. For the mystery reader, the Hitchcock film contained a number of disappointments, mainly in the fact that the surprise solution is revealed too early, unlike *Diabolique*, which saves some of its shocks for the end. But there can be no faulting Hitchcock's technique, and some critics believe *Vertigo* to be his most fully realized masterpiece.

The most popular of Hitchcock's films was *Psycho* (1960), based on Robert Bloch's novel of the same title. Although the film sale earned Bloch very little money, it brought him lasting fame and proved to be a cinematic milestone, unleashing a decade of psychopathic horror films. The film is generally faithful to the book, although the book opens from the viewpoint of Norman Bates rather than Mary Crane, the girl who becomes the first victim. And the murder in the shower features a beheading that Hitchcock wisely omitted.

The next film from Hitchcock, and the last of his big successes, was *The Birds* (1963). Based on a short story by Daphne du Maurier that furnished little more than the general idea and ending, the film must really be viewed as the work of screenwriter Evan Hunter, with liberal doses of Hitchcockian technique.

As a general rule, in these films and all his others, Hitchcock took more liberties with his source material than most other directors. But the liberties were almost always concerned with technique or with the necessities of the marketplace. Although authors might complain about their treatment by Hollywood or the amount of money they were paid, it's doubtful that many of them were dissatisfied with the end result of a Hitchcock adaptation. In most cases he produced a film that was equal or superior to the story on which it was based.

The 1940s saw a number of other fine mystery films that helped establish the fame of the novels on which they were based. Vera Caspery's *Laura* was filmed in 1944 by Otto Preminger. While remaining faithful to the book, Preminger improved on it in several small ways—the hiding place of the murder weapon, for instance. The book, good as it is, suffers somewhat from an awkward use of shifting first-person narration, with first Waldo, then Lieutenant McPherson, and then Laura herself taking up the story. Such a technique was automatically eliminated from a film version, and the main plot line flowed more smoothly, helped immeasurably by fine background music.

Likewise, the 1944 film version of Eric Ambler's *The Mask of Dimitrios*, with a screenplay by American mystery writer Frank Gruber, helped establish Ambler as a master of international intrigue. It was especially remarkable for its time in that no romance was added to the plot to fit popular stars. The cast was composed mainly of character actors who carried the action very well. It was a faithful rendering that showed romance was not an essential element of the mystery-intrigue film.

Before we leave the 1940s, something should be said about the series detectives who occupied the bottom half of double bills. They all but disappeared in the 1950s with the coming of television, but in the postwar years they were still around. Some have been mentioned earlier in comments about series which grew from single stories, but there were others whose creators turned out a large body of adventures for them. Often they did not fare well on film. The movie Nick Carter, for instance, was an updated detective who bore not the slightest resemblance to the dime-novel sleuth of the same name. Basil Rathbone and Nigel Bruce made their first appearances as Sherlock Holmes and Dr. Watson in a fine 1939 version of *The Hound of the Baskervilles*, moodily faithful to the flavor if not the letter of Conan Doyle's text. But after one more period piece, *The Adventures of Sherlock Holmes*, the series was modernized, no doubt for budget reasons, and relegated to the bottom half of double bills. Although some of the resulting films were enjoyable enough, they weren't really about the Holmes and Watson we'd come to love through the books.

Charlie Chan fared somewhat better in the long series of films based on Earl Derr Biggers's character. Oddly enough, the early silent films taken from the first three novels altered and minimized Chan's role. He is listed twelfth in the cast of *The House without a Key*, a 1926 serial, and makes only a token appearance at the end of *Behind That Curtain* (1929). Even in *Charlie Chan Carries On*, the first Chan talking film and a close adaptation of the book, Warner Oland's Chan appears only in the final portion of the plot. This was, of course, true of most of Biggers's books, which usually opened with other characters carrying the action until Chan appeared. Only in the last of Biggers's six Chan novels, *Keeper of the Keys* (1932), does Charlie himself appear in the opening scene, although *Charlie Chan Carries On* opens with a Scotland Yard inspector receiving a letter from him. Thus, movie audiences usually saw more of the famed detective in the string of second features using the character—more, perhaps, than his creator had intended.

A full decade passed after the first of Leslie Charteris's books about the Saint before the character was translated to the screen in *The Saint in New York* (1938), but a string of generally successful films followed. A few were based on the Charteris books, but more used the character in new adventures in typical B picture fashion. Still, the Saint was one of the few movie detectives to make a successful later transition to television, and 114 hour-long episodes were aired between 1963 and 1968.

The 1950s marked the real birth of television for the masses, and as we indicated earlier, the second-feature movie series faded before the growth of television series. Characters such as Ellery Queen, who had had indifferent success on the big screen, starred in various weekly series, some based on the original Queen novels. In fact, when Queen's *The Glass Village* (1954), one of the few novels without the Ellery Queen character, was shown on television, Ellery was substituted for the original detective.

The Ellery Queen character did not always do so well on television, however. A 1971 adaptation of *Cat of Many Tails*, one of the classic Queen novels, transformed Ellery's father to his uncle and gave him an unfamiliar British accent in the person of Peter Lawford in the starring role. Much of the book's power, dealing with New York's hysterical reaction to a baffling series of strangulations, is dissipated in this version, awkwardly titled *Ellery Queen: Don't Look Behind You*. A drawing of a cat with nooses for tails, which became a symbol of the killer in the book, was dropped from television in favor of a snake, apparently so as not to offend cat-lovers.

Ellery fared better in a 1975 television adaptation of *The Fourth Side of the Triangle*, although the TV film was meticulously set in the 1940s, whereas the original novel had a contemporary setting when published in 1965. Star Jim Hutton went on to play Ellery in a weekly series for which this served as the pilot. The stories were well-clued mysteries but for the most part were not based on the original Queen books.

The only mystery film with a series detective ever to win an Academy Award for best picture of the year was *In the Heat of the Night* (1967). (Other winners with more than a touch of mystery included *Rebecca*, *The Godfather*, and *The Sting*.) This first adventure of John Ball's black detective Virgil Tibbs made a compelling motion picture, even though some slight changes were made in the plot. Tibbs, a Pasadena homicide detective in the book, becomes a Philadelphia detective in the film. Since both book and movie are set in a small Southern town, Tibbs's home hardly seems that important, and one wonders why the change was made. Two later Tibbs films were not based on Ball's books and were less successful.

The *Godfather* was perhaps the best example during the 1970s of how a bestselling crime novel could be faithfully and powerfully adapted for the screen. If some incidents, flashbacks, and subplots had to be trimmed from the lengthy novel, these were mostly covered in the sequel to the film, and both films were combined for television as a mini-series. The author, Mario Puzo, and the viewers were well served by director Francis Ford Coppola, and one reason for this successful adaptation must surely lie in the fact that the original author and the director collaborated on the screenplay.

The spy film, which has had its ups and downs in Hollywood, always seems to be better made in England, just as the best espionage novelists are, almost without exception, British. Graham Greene fared especially well in adaptations of his work, possibly because he was often involved as screenwriter. Even since the filming of *Orient Express* in 1934, Greene's work has been turned into a series of evocative films. *This Gun For Hire* (1942), *The Ministry of Fear* (1943), *Confidential Agent* (1945), and *Brighton Rock* (1946) all captured the mood of the books admirably while sometimes deviating from individual plot points. Greene's own willingness to recognize the differences between books and films can be seen in comparing the printed and movie versions of *The Third Man*, Greene's 1949 masterpiece of intrigue in postwar Vienna. Greene wrote the short novel only as a preliminary step to the screenplay, without any intention of publishing it. Although he has written that the novelist "cannot help resenting many of the changes necessary for turning [his book] into a film play," Greene admits to making changes in *The Third Man* himself to better adapt it to the screen. And he credits Carol Reed, the director, with suggesting the proper downbeat ending to the film's romantic subplot.

But in one area the films of Greene's work have almost completely ignored their source material. The religious aspect of his characters, present even in books like *This Gun For Hire*, usually vanished from the film versions. Perhaps that is why a movie like *True Confessions* (1981), adapted by John Gregory Dunne and his wife Joan Didion from Dunne's novel, is so successful. It has the courage to mix religion and murder, a mixture that has frightened earlier generations of producers and editors.

If Greene's religious views frightened the filmmakers, so did his political views. The 1957 film version of *The Quiet American* had its ironic ending reemphasized in such a way that the film became anti-Communist while the book was anti-American, at least regarding America's role in the Far East. The latest Greene novel to be filmed, *The Human Factor*, follows its source exactly, although it is not as successful as the book.

But the spy films of the 1960s and 1970s were more likely to feature a James Bond sort of hero than the melancholy protagonists of Greene's books. As they increased in box-office popularity, the Bond films moved further away from Ian Fleming's novels into a world of stylized gimmickry where the goal seemed merely to top the sensations of the previous Bond film. Beginning with *Dr. No* in 1963, a faithful adaptation of the book, they progressed to *The Spy Who Loved Me*, *Moonraker*, and *For Your Eyes Only*, in which nothing of Fleming's books remained except the titles.

The harsh realism of *The Spy Who Came in from the Cold*, directed by Martin Ritt in 1965 from John Le Carré's bestselling novel, was a welcome relief from Bond. But although the well-acted film was faithful to its source, the harsh, grainy black-and-white photography added too much of a downbeat note to a story that hardly needed it. Le Carré was better served by the 1980 television mini-series of *Tinker*, *Tailor*, *Soldier*, *Spy*.

If the film versions of Fleming and Le Carré followed in the wake of their popular books, the movie adaptation of Len Deighton's *The Ipcress File* (1965) was so successful that it made Michael Caine a star and lifted the Deighton book from obscurity. Deighton's American publisher had bypassed his second novel, *Horse Under Water*, and it remained unpublished in the United States for five years. But his third and fourth books, *Funeral in Berlin* (1964) and *The Billion Dollar Brain*

(1966), proved popular here and were filmed as sequels to *The Ipcress File*. The main difference between the films and the books is that Deighton's nameless, reluctant spy became "Harry Palmer" on the screen.

The film and television adaptations of my own short stories—more than a dozen at this writing—have followed familiar routes. One story was expanded to make a feature-length film shown mainly on television in this country. Called *It Takes All Kinds*, it used my story for its first half, climaxing in a museum robbery, and then followed the characters through their trackdown and ultimate capture by police—something I had not done in my story.

Three other stories, adapted for the television series *McMillan & Wife*, were reasonably faithful to my plots but changed the characters to fit the demands of the continuing series. Another story, written in a realistic style, became a fantasy about the devil when adapted for the series *Night Gallery*. Perhaps the most successful adaptations from my point of view have been two stories done by the British syndicated series *Tales of the Unexpected*. I like them because they remain the closest to the stories as I wrote them.

It is a difficult thing for an author to see his or her work tampered with in another medium. Perhaps all of us share something of the resentment mentioned by Graham Greene when even necessary changes are made. We wish for a film as fine and as faithful to us as Huston's *Maltese Falcon* was to Hammett. More often, we end with something far removed from what we have written, and we watch the images on the screen as if they were the work of a stranger.

As indeed they are.

10

Writers on Their Mysterious Calling

Eleanor Sullivan

The question is as old as the hills. Why do writers write?

In *About Fiction* (1975), Wright Morris says, "Before they made tools, before they made trouble, men and women were busy at the loom of fiction looking for clues to becoming more human."

William Maxwell told Bob Dahlin for *Publishers Weekly*: "Perhaps it's essentially a maternal thing to want to make life acceptable. You know how a mother comforts a child who's come up against the world. Perhaps my writing is the ghost of my mother working through me."

Graham Greene compares it to religion: "Like a Catholic priest, writers are unfulfilled. The priest cannot get close enough to sanctity in his own eyes. The writer cannot get close enough to writing well."

Journalist and writer Shaun Usher/Jeffry Scott was attracted to the life by his parents, both of whom wrote: "But my folks never told me that writing wasn't that easy, that it's fraught with as many rebuffs as those facing a not very pretty hooker with a sensitive nature working a bad convention. There can't be many other trades where you offer the best you've got to total strangers, who need to feel no compunction about telling you to get lost."

"I sometimes think," Edna O'Brien confessed in a self-interview in *Playboy* some years ago, "that writers are the great pretenders of all time. They feel everything both more and less. Without question, they are split people, experiencing and observing at one and the same time. To tell you the truth, I would rather be a witch or a dancer or a shepherdess."

Does it ever get any easier? If you care about what you're writing, it would seem not.

S. J. Perelman said, "The old apothegm that easy writing makes hard reading is as succinct as ever."

Thomas Lask quoted Harry Kemelman, author of the Rabbi series, in the *New York Times*: "My method of writing is trial and error. I have a feeling, an emotion, a crazy little idea, not a story or plot. Who would say it? Whom would he say it to? I start working that out. But after seventy pages I feel I'm on the wrong track. Two other characters should have said it. So I start again. I do that five, seven, maybe eight times, until by brute force I get through to the end of the story. That makes up my first draft. If there are 2,000 words left from the first in the final draft, I'm lucky."

When I was with Scribner's as an editor, I copy-edited the mammoth, exquisite novel *Miss MacIntosh, My Darling*. The 3,449-page typescript had taken Marguerite Young seventeen years to complete. "I was never bored for a moment in the writing of it," she said. "I wrote every day, seven hours a day, including the Fourth of July. Maybe once in three or four years I would go uptown for lunch."

In an article in *The Atlantic*, John Kenneth Galbraith commented: "All writers know that on some golden mornings they are touched by the wand—are on intimate terms with poetry and cosmic truth. I have experienced those moments myself. Their lesson is simple: It's a total illusion. And the danger in the illusion is that you will wait for those moments. Such is the horror of having to face the typewriter that you will spend all your time waiting. I am persuaded that most writers, like most shoemakers, are about as good one day as the next [and] one had better go to his or her typewriter every morning and stay there regardless of the seeming result. It will be much the same."

So much for the agony of writing. Here are some answers from writers regarding how they happened into mystery writing and their feelings about the genre and their craft.

Christianna Brand told Otto Penzler for *Ellery Queen's Mystery Magazine* (hereafter to be referred to as *EQMM*): "I hated a girl I worked with in a shop, and it was a sublimation, I suppose—now that we use these grand words—of my anything *but* subconscious wish to murder her."

P. D. James, in an interview with Carla Heffner in *The Washington Post*, said: "I believe one reason women dominate the genre is their love of order. Murder creates disorder and finding the murderer restores order. Also, women understand personal feelings like jealousy and hatred. They are more interested in violent emotions than in violent crimes, and so you have the 'gentle' art of murder—poison rather than guns, kitchen knives rather than high explosive."

"I believe," Patricia Highsmith told me for *EQMM*, "that coincidences turn up pretty frequently in life, or in reality, so I don't know why any writer would rule them out of his work. I am fond of what I call a wild coincidence in my stories. I think it worked in *The Blunderer*. . . . It is not a question of fairness [to the reader] but of credibility."

"I just loathe it when an author has to force a murderer to confess," Mignon G. Eberhart was quoted by Jean Mercier in *Publishers Weekly*. "I always try to evolve jury evidence—it's one of the demands I make on myself: the denouement must be incontrovertible evidence that a district attorney can use."

Dorothy Salisbury Davis told *Publishers Weekly*'s Barbara Bannon: "Any art is contrived: the degree of artistry lies in how you conceal that contrivance. You are guaranteed to have to write in a bizarre fashion for mysteries. Something violent has to happen, something that is not expected, something that is showy. Being bizarre means color, too, and I like that."

"If I do create good and sympathetic characters," Thomas Walsh replied to my question in *EQMM*, "I think it's because of the slowness of pace with which I write, so that I never start a yarn before I feel close as a brother to the people involved. I count no man frailer than myself, as I think Thomas à Kempis wrote, and I suppose this has always given me a head start in the right direction."

Asked about his series character, nightclub owner-comedian Chick Kelly, S. S. Rafferty said: "While I'm sure there's something of me in Chick, Chick is not me. If I identified with him too much there would be things I wouldn't let him do, and that would be death for the series."

"I think fine old movies are great for a writer to look at and ponder over," Robert Twohy said. "They're basic story technique, which applies to any fiction: quick and sure characterization, hang out a story line, stay tight to it, and keep out of the way. Those movies packed

in the fans because the writers knew how to grab, entertain, excite—
and how to keep things moving."

Patricia Moyes told me: "The fashion world is no place for a writer,
but I'm grateful to it for giving me a job when I needed one, and for
imposing a rigid discipline on my writing. I envied, but never had, the
instinctive flair for fashion possessed by my colleagues in the Fashion
Room—they simply *knew* when a look was right or wrong. Today, one
of my greatest friends is an ex-colleague from *Vogue*, and she can look
more stunningly stylish in an old raincoat than I ever could, even if
all my clothes came from the greatest Paris houses. Like writing, this
is a mysterious gift."

Said Joyce Porter: "I grew up in the great age of detective-story
writing, just before World War II, and read them avidly. Nowadays,
for obvious reasons, I don't. I'm terrified of being halfway through
writing a book and then reading one on the same theme. I make an
exception for foreign ones though, especially Emma Lathen."

Emma Lathen is, of course, the pseudonym for the two anonymous
authors of the John Putnam Thatcher/Sloan Guaranty Trust novels
(*Pick Up Sticks*, 1970; *Ashes to Ashes*, 1971, etc.). Several years ago they
told *Harvard Magazine*, "A couple of times we created a foolproof murder that not even Thatcher could solve, and we had to go back and put
in a mistake or two on the part of the murderer."

I've loved interviews for so long—those in print perhaps even more
than those on television, radio, and the lecture platform—that it was
simply a matter of time and opportunity before I took interviewing up
myself. Because of geographical distance from most of the writers I've
interviewed for *EQMM*, however, most of the interviews have been by
mail. This being so, they may lack the livelier exchanges that are possible face to face, but that isn't the fault of the subjects, who have
responded with the spirit and personality that have distinguished them
as writers.

Janwillem van de Wetering (*The Japanese Corpse*, 1977; *The Maine
Massacre*, 1979): "*Do* I have a sense of humor? You said it, not me. My
easy relatability—again your term—must, if indeed I have it, be due
to traveling and group effort under adverse circumstances. If you can't
join them, you can always try to lick them. Relatability is a Dutch
characteristic, according to our own history books, which are slanted

to enlarge our egos. According to this theory we became adaptable because we had to—there was the sea on one side and enemies on the other."

Lillian de la Torre, creator of the Dr. Sam: Johnson detective stories and a number of books and plays, including *Goodbye, Miss Lizzie Borden*: "When young director Joseph L. Mankiewicz read my first true-crime book, *Elizabeth Is Missing*, a tale of kidnapping and bawdry on the seamy side of London in 1752, he sent for me in a hurry. 'I want to do a remake of *Berkeley Square*,' he said. 'You remember how at the climax of the play the time-traveller looks out on the Square and exclaims in disgust, *God, how the eighteenth century stinks*. You're here to put in the stinks.' He handed me a draft of his script, and I put in the stinks. Joe never did make *Berkeley Square*, which is a pity, for he had a wonderful gimmick for giving life to that old chestnut."

Jack Ritchie, master of the humorous short story and winner of this year's Edgar from the Mystery Writers of America for his story "The Absence of Emily," *EQMM*, January 28, 1981: "The short story seems to be my field, possibly by forfeit. I've always felt that there hasn't been a novel published that couldn't be reduced to a better short story. Often the very long novels are really collections of short stories and sometimes they even include what are basically articles. Victor Hugo was good at that. He put about 30,000 words into *Les Miserables* delineating the history, structure, and whatnot of the Paris sewers. Now if I'd been in his shoes I could have described the sewers in two paragraphs. Maybe one. *Les Miserables* itself would have become a novelette. Possibly even a pamphlet."

Michael Gilbert, author of countless superb novels, short stories, and plays: "The best description of courage I ever read was in a letter to the [London] *Times* from Bernard Shaw at a moment when people were pouring out a lot of rather silly adulation on the captain of *The Titanic*. I cannot give it to you verbatim, but what he saw was that courage was the expression of a fine character in action in adverse circumstances. Surrounding circumstances such as darkness, storms, and a waste of waters might heighten the dramatic effect but they were nothing to do with the actions themselves. He added that all the captain had really done was run into an iceberg. This annoyed other correspondents a lot."

Clark Howard (*American Saturday*, winner of last year's MWA Edgar for "Horn Man," *EQMM*, June 6, 1981): "I literally grew up in the [Marine] Corps. Many of my personal values, my extreme neatness, my ability to organize, my self-confidence, were all learned in the Corps. It was my family and teacher during some very important years. I served in Korea as a rocket launcher gunner—was with a unit decorated by President Truman for holding the high ground north of the Punch-bowl for 200 consecutive days. I spent my eighteenth birthday in Japan on the way back from Korea."

Novelist and short story and screenwriter George Baxt: "New York is my first home and always will be. Today it's dirty, squalid, and still more exhilarating than suicide. But I'd prefer to be in London. . . . My one desire is to return and live and die there. I wish to be cremated at Golders Green Crematorium—which isn't far from where Jack the Ripper operated."

Philip Atkey, aka Barry Perowne, author of the present series of stories about jewel thief and amateur cracksman A. J. Raffles, origi-nated by E. W. Hornung: "In my very early days in Fleet Street, I saw the unmistakable figure of Chesterton looming up hugely in a dense fog. He was wearing a broad-brimmed felt hat and a cloak like a mat-ador's. He was silhouetted against the lights in the window of a phren-ologist's shop, scribbling away on the back of an envelope pressed to the window. Can he have been writing a piece on phrenology for his *Daily News* column or for his own *G.K.'s Weekly?* I still wonder."

I was hardly the first to conduct interviews by mail. One of the best of its kind I've read was conducted from the Federal penitentiary in Marion, Illinois, by the prolific writer of mystery short stories Al Nussbaum, who was then serving a forty-year sentence for armed bank robbery. His subject was Donald E. Westlake, author of many highly successful caper novels, including *Cops and Robbers* (1972), for which he also wrote the screenplay. The periodical was *Take One*.

In his introduction to the interview, Nussbaum explained, "I wrote [Westlake] a letter, modestly explaining that I was probably the person best qualified to interview him. 'I'm in prison, and the consensus is that you should be. You have a far too devious mind to be allowed to run free.'"

In the course of the delicious interview, Westlake said, "In writing books, of course, what you do is more important than how often you've done it, but in writing screenplays a credit is better than no credit at all. That you've written a piece of shit that got made is one up for you; that you've written three beauties that have not been made is three down for you. If a producer gets his projects made, what more can you want from the man? . . .

"I heard this exchange of dialogue between Elliott [Kastner] and another producer at dinner one night: Other producer: 'You ever get that tax problem straightened out?' Kastner: 'All but a hundred fifty thousand of it.' I wish I could write dialogue like that.

"Early in our relationship, Kastner said these two sentences to me in a row very earnestly and seriously: 'I've made seventeen pictures in six years. I've never made a picture I didn't care about.' Saint Francis of Assisi couldn't care about seventeen pictures in six years."

Most interviews we see in print have been conducted, briefly or at length—sometimes great length, over a number of days—face to face. This is a different art for both interviewer and subject, and the success of the interviews depends largely on the motivations of the two parties as well as their mood at the time(s) of confrontation. The interviewer may have a lot riding on the interview, the subject may not, or vice versa. It's not necessarily a bad thing. If both do, that too may not be a bad thing. If neither does, that may not be a bad thing. But any one of these chemistries can certainly be unfortunate. Then too, either or both may be under pressure or talked out or answerable to others for his or her questions or answers, with hedging and hostility the result rather than enlightenment and laughter. Whatever the interviewer and interviewee can do to make the venture helpful rather than hurtful to themselves and their reading audience should be the objective; otherwise, better not do it.

There is a continuing quandary regarding "live" print interviews— whether to use a tape recorder or rely on notes and memory. Helen Ruttencutter, author of several beautifully detailed *New Yorker* profiles, is in favor of the tape recorder for accuracy, especially when talking to specialists. This is presuming that they will allow one and that you are in agreement that certain confidences are off the record.

Don Bensen interviewed Rex Stout for *Writer's Digest* in 1968 and P. G. Wodehouse for the same magazine in 1971. For the earlier interview he didn't use a tape recorder; for the later one he did. The taped interview with Wodehouse, he feels, had less flavor than the one with Stout, quite possibly because of the different techniques used. But the notepad approach, he recalls, was a great strain, and the fictional element involved in reconstructing the conversation was something he wasn't entirely comfortable with. Nevertheless, he had both authors' approval of what went into the magazine. A sample of each follows:

Stout: "Nearly all the works of fiction done in the last thirty years that I'm personally glad to have read are detective stories. Most of what are called writers of serious fiction now seem to be convinced not that this or that man or woman is bad, say, but that life itself is unacceptable. Well, I certainly do not believe that life is unacceptable. Some people, of course, are unacceptable."

Wodehouse: "My great rule is that I do think you have to be an absolutely impartial critic of your own stuff. When you've got a thing down on paper, you've got to read it just as if it was somebody else's work and you were criticizing it. Otherwise you're apt to get things in that ought not to be there."

In my own live interviewing for print, I've used a tape recorder at times and a notepad at others. While I agree that working from notes can be a strain and that the tape recorder is more accurate, I found using tape more time-consuming without appreciably different results. It is, of course, nice to have the interview tapes for posterity if, unlike me, you can bear listening to the sound of your own voice and your gaffes. All things considered, I prefer the mail interview. That way both parties have plenty of time to think over their questions and answers without getting out of their bathrobes if they don't want to.

This morning's mail brought a letter from Robert B. Parker (*A Savage Place* and *Ceremony*), to whom I'd sent a battery of questions for an interview with him in *EQMM*.

"Working on your questionnaire. It will be in the mail in a week or two—love the topic."

So do I.

11

The Truth, More or Less, as Long as It Makes a Good Story

Shannon OCork

If, long ago, back in Lyndon, Kentucky, where I was born, I murdered Johnny Williams and got away with it, I could not admit it now, could I? The case is still on the books there in Jefferson County, and in Kentucky there is no statute of limitation on murder. But maybe I did. I wrote a novel about it once. Or, better, maybe I can make you think I did. I'd like to put the possibility of it and a little suspicion in your mind. The truth of the matter, as truth usually is, is a mix of fact and fancy. Of reportage and fiction. Truman Capote says all novelists are liars. And I say all big lies begin with little truths.

Johnny Williams was twenty-two years old in 1959. Curly-haired. Golden-chested. He died in Lover's Hollow alongside Beargrass Creek. He was stabbed with a potato knife. Within two minutes, his blue eyes faded to gray. A potato knife is a sharp, long-bladed knife used in the field to cut potatoes out of the ground, cut them free from the earth-loving roots that can run deep as coffins. And be hard to cut through as bone. Everyone said Johnny's girl friend, Margaret Mary Dillman, did it. She didn't. Monsignor Roland started that rumor. Margaret Mary was pregnant and she was shamed. She ran away after. I heard she never did come back. Isabelle Williams, Johnny's sister, said she'd wait for Margaret Mary. Swore she'd be layin' for her. Far as I know, and it's been years now, Izzard still is. Izzard always was mean-spirited like that; the kind of person who thought *The Ox-Bow Incident* was a comedy. I was only fifteen years old at the time, but I remember it well. In my time around Lyndon, Kay-wy, the killing of Johnny Williams was the biggest thing ever happened.

To write the story of Johnny Williams's murder, I'd re-create the characters, the situation, and the scene as exactly as I could. That's called focusing, locating the event precisely where you want it. I'd intensify a few details and eliminate those that didn't affect the story. I'd add in, painterly, some chosen-for-effect touches. I'd want to make dramatic the reason I killed Johnny, and I'd want you to like him and care that he died. I'd want you to like me, too, the narrator-character and murderer. So, through the writing, I'd lace in reader wooing; that is, I'd talk to you confidentially, one on one, as to a friend. That's likable, and I'd hope you wouldn't notice it was purposeful.

I'd keep the year it happened the same as it really was, 1959, so that everything I remembered would fit properly into the time. When I think of the summer Johnny Williams died, here are some of the things I remember, fresh as mint at Derbytime: the general store-post office in Lyndon, and Mrs. Ada Guthrie, and the exotic look of a first-class stamp. The signs that cautioned us from riding the horses on the new, concrete sidewalks along Beech Drive into town. The ice house. What we talked about at supper. How we prayed. The limestone quarry where Johnny used to meet my mama, other side of Beargrass Creek, other side of Lover's Hollow. The action of the novel would take place among those remembered things. The things time, not people, change. The things that change when you aren't looking, the things you didn't realize were special and one-time-only until after they are gone for good and final. In writing, it's called putting in the local color. It's particularizing the environment.

Since I would be looking back, I could foreshadow events to come. And if I wanted, I'd be able to prophesy. That's called narrator omniscience or less grandly, Monday-morning quarterbacking.

I'd not forget the *telling detail*, the particular and peculiar characteristics of a time or a place or a character. One telling detail I'd use would be the dress I wore the night Johnny died; its collar, and how it tore on the knot of barbed wire, and what that meant after.

There was a long way and a short way to Bickel's quarry. The shortcut was through our cow pasture. That night I was bellying under the barbed-wire fence, looking for my mama. I saw Johnny up the hill of the hollow, in the pussy willow weeds with Margaret Mary. I forgot

I was still stretched under the bottom strand. I lifted my head and caught my collar behind on a wire knot, on the three spiny barbs they leave sticking out to turn the cow back if she leans on the fencing too hard.

The reason the torn collar was important was because Auntie 'Phine always starched my collars and cuffs too much. One of the things I hated about Sacred Heart Academy was having to peel open the starched breast pocket of my white uniform blouse every Monday morning when I dressed. The whole blouse felt like cardboard until Friday, and Friday nights it got washed and starched again. And long before my dresses wore out, the collars frayed and the cuffs cracked. I'd have to go on wearing the dresses that way because they were basically still good. When I complained, Auntie 'Phine said pride was a devil's toy, but it was her lack of understanding of a young girl and her dresses that was the problem, not my pride. I begged her every time, "Please, Auntie, no starch." The reader would want to know about the overstarching because it was a *telling detail* in the killing of Johnny. It was what made no one think of me as anything other than an innocent witness to an especially savage murder.

Of course, I'd have to explain how that all worked out. It would be one of the *plot devices* in the novel, a thread of continuity. And I could use it to show character: Auntie 'Phine starching collars and cuffs was scary. She was dedicated to her task. (Give her any worthy task and she would quickly grow dedicated to it. You should have seen her on Sunday mornings, listening to Mass on the radio, gutting the dinner chicken with her bare hands.)

Auntie 'Phine was righteous as only a country virgin spinster can be. She liked the *Jack Benny Show*, but she had no sense of humor. What she had was a dressing mirror, oval, and rosewood, and tall as I was. In the evenings after prayers, Auntie 'Phine would go into the front parlor room Dad converted into her and Aunt Agnes's bedroom. (Twin beds and, between, a statue of the bleeding heart of Jesus on a round oak table, a votary candle burning before in a thick, blood-red glass. The statue stood on a doily starched stiff enough to cut your fingers.) Auntie 'Phine would sit herself on the piano stool in front of the mirror and brush her never-cut gray hair. The hair was long as Rapunzel's. Auntie 'Phine would sit a long time, counting brushstrokes in whispers, smiling at something inside the mirror only she could see. I asked her once if she'd ever had a lover. Aunt Agnes heard. She beat me until the yardstick broke.

What I've done here is called *character delineation*. Through visual description, if I did it right, the reader caught a glimpse of Auntie 'Phine's soul. At its best, character delineation should be *heuristic*; that is, it should interest the reader and lead him or her to read on and learn more.

The story would have a provincial period flavor, then, of the American South in the late 1950s. For the action scenes, I would want *immediacy*; a you-are-there feeling for the reader. I would not want the novel to read like history. I'd want the reader to follow the fifteen-year-old girl, the first-person narrator. I'd want the reader to mentally participate in her emotions and actions and reactions. I'd want the reader, male or female, to *identify*.

To get *immediacy*, vividness, into the murder scene, I'd use Roysie and what happened to him last August. Roysie's stabbing is still startling in my mind. The killing of Johnny has grown warm and soft like a favorite blanket; I've slept with the killing of Johnny for a long, long time. I'd merge the two actual crimes into one fictional one. I'd work out the sequence of events of what happened to Johnny, and exactly how. That would be the *plot*. And then I'd overlay the stabbing of Roysie, about which I learned through effective *reportage*.

That way, I'll get the *objective* and the *subjective* together. I'll lace how it was (the objective) with how it looked (the subjective). They'll form a pattern, called the *author's style*.

I'll try to stay away from the *banal* and the *extraneous*. An example of the banal would be what my sister said when she heard about the death of Johnny. She said something forgettable like: "Gee, and he was so cute, too. Conceited, but cute."

An example of the extraneous would be whoever was walking on the other side of the street when Roysie was borne that night, under a bloodied white sheet, out of our apartment building on a stretcher by paramedics. There was no moon. The sheet glowed astrally in the mercury-green of the streetlamps. On the stretcher, Roysie sat straight as a corpse coming out of rigor mortis. He said to me, me just out of a cab and dumbfounded: "Hope *you* had a nice night, dear." He was smoking a Marlboro. He was naked and white as Moby Dick. His hair hugged his forehead in sweaty little wisps. His face was the color of

wet concrete. Roysie was slid, then, like a greased thermometer, into
the gray anus of the ambulance. The ambulance door closed, quiet.
The people on the other side of the street and what they thought, for
this scene, are *extraneous*. They are without importance or effect. This
scene is about Roysie, and, underneath, about Roysie and me.

Roysie is my neighbor. He lives just above me with his roommate,
Morris, in 2-A. Roysie will tell you: "When I want to be, I'm the
sweetest person in the world." Usually, when I'm sweet (unless I love
you) it's because I'm after something I can use in my fiction. I'm after
reportage. I want to yank away at a life and hold the vital parts of it in
the long claws of my memory. And then use it sometime in the telling
of a tale. And so it was that I got sweet with Roysie last August.

It was about 1 A.M. of a muggy, cloud-hiding-moon, hot Wednes-
day. Roysie was mugged in his apartment. Roysie had the top window
open and the air conditioner on full. He fell asleep on the blue velvet
sofa waiting for Morris to get home from Roosevelt Hospital, where
Morris works as a nurse's aid. All Roysie was wearing were his favorite
jogging shorts, the pink satin ones with the little slits on the thighs,
and his tank watch from Cartier. And a little Royal Copenhagen, which
was no help at all, he said.

Apartments 1-A and 2-A of the brownstone where we live face
the street behind a curlicued wrought-iron fence. A young black man,
a teenager really, Roysie and the witnesses agree, climbed from the
fence to the lintel of the door of the attached apartment house next to
us. From the arch there, the burglar long-stepped to the ledge under
the second-story windows of our place. Then, one sneaker on the air
conditioner box and up. He slithered into Roysie's apartment through
the open top window. Roysie was robbed, of course. Worse, he was
slashed deeply in the abdomen, down and into the lower intestine. The
gouge in the bowel alone took ninety minutes of surgery to repair.
When I asked, concerned friend of Roysie's that I was, the doctor
explained it to me: The bowel is round and slippery, and the tear was
long and jagged-lipped and uneven. Roysie's thigh was sliced to the
bone. The femoral artery was severed. This is what almost killed him.
Roysie remembers the attack. Remembers his blood spurting from his
thigh like sap out of a ripe maple tree. The blood was astonishingly
red, he says, and thick, and full of life.

Seeing his own blood, Roysie says, excited him. His attacker was small and young. Almost frail, Roysie said. As I, arms curved like scimitars, out of my dress collar caught on the barbed wire, must have seemed frail and harmless, running toward Johnny. Johnny's eyes had been on my white, dressless body and not on the potato knife he himself had sharpened for me the day before on the flintstone wheel behind the barn.

Roysie says he struck with his fist, that he was bigger, but with the knife his assailant was better. "He cut me down," Roysie told me, "as I flailed at him. Attacking, he never said a word. His breath in my ear was terrifying; rhythmic and muffling, like water rushing over me. And then there was a pounding in my head that was my blood pulsing out of my body." I listened carefully. Later, alone, I made notes. *Reportage.*

After his attacker left, Roysie came out on the between-floor landing. His life was bleeding away. He lit a cigarette, a Marlboro. Roysie was high from shock or loss of blood. He is not sure why, but he was euphoric, he said, beyond pain and into celestial pleasure. He sang, a capella, Kenny Rogers's "The Gambler." The mugger had cut the telephone cord, cut the curled cord between the receiver and the body of the telephone. So Roysie stumbled out onto the first-floor landing, starkers in his ripped satin boxers, bloody as Julius Caesar. Singing country and calling for me.

He got no answer. While Roysie was being ravaged, I was downtown. At Sardi's. Being rushed by a Hollywood producer's talent scout, who wanted, for a kiss and a promise, the film rights to a novel I'd written. I was sipping anisette and Colombian espresso slicked with lemon oil. Talking the big money. Getting stroked. Feeling wonderful.

The night Johnny was murdered, the potato knife found his heart. Veins, not arteries, were cut. Veins do not gush with pent-up force as arteries do. Veins take the blood toward the heart and lungs, and the color of the blood is not so brilliantly crimson. Arteries carry the blood away. Arterial blood is fresh with oxygen and very red and explosive when freed.

Learning these biologic facts, if one did not know them before and wants to use them in a story for *authenticity* or for *effect*, is called *research*. *Authenticity* in fiction is writing with probability on your side, writing as close to actuality as one is able to. *Effect* is, simply, emphasis. Effect is tricky, though, because it can tilt a story all the way from serious to funny.

My writing is deceptively simple. It looks easy until the reader gets into it. And then the writing winds, gracefully devious, and slithers off to strange places. Like a diamondback rattler, or so I like to think. (This is called *self-confidence*. In the writing game you cannot have too much of it.) So for me, things like *authenticity* and *effect* and *research* are best when they are simple. Simple and vivid. If the research is too complicated, the story either gets lost in the research or the story is being written by the wrong writer. There will ever be stories, good stories, that are not for me. I leave them despite their temptation. One was a beauty, the story of a Scots woman who killed her husband. He stayed away too long on offshore oil rigs in the North Sea. He did it for love of her. For the extra money. Because he did it, she grew to hate him. Cooked him a carrot souffle and put him in the ground. The tale was mine for the asking, and it had the black humor I like and the irony. The contract was generous: carte blanche, within reason, on expenses. I would go to the town for research and reportage. But it would have meant, for me, too much of both. I did not know the territory, hers or his. I would have come, and stayed, a stranger. The story, in my hands, would not have been as wonderful as it could be. Some day it will get told, better told, by someone else.

For simple things, one can consult an expert, in which case one has a *source*, an authority in the field or in that area of expertise. I file my sources in a *source book* and remember the persons from time to time. This is called keeping one's contacts open. To have an open contact is to have *access*, and *access* is what all storytelling, *reportage* (which is supposed to be true), and *fiction* (which is supposed to be imaginary) is based on. Whether you are creating or reporting, access to a story is the crucial first door if the story is not your own. This is why writers write so often in the first person. We always have access to ourselves.

When Johnny was stabbed, he was lying on his back in brown Kentucky grass, surrounded by pussy willows. His blood did not spurt like Roysie's. Johnny's blood seeped like tidewater over his white T-shirt, like a huge ketchup mistake for Rosie, the quicker picker-upper, to wipe up with her Bounty paper towels. After Johnny was stabbed,

I dreamed of mopping up Johnny's blood with Bounties, and the paper towels finally shredding from the effort the way, in the TV ads, the competition's do. Brand X. Or did the dreams come later, long later, after I went away. After I knew Margaret Mary had been blamed and would never come back and that they wouldn't chase her and hound her home. They knew she would come to a bad end. Everyone who knew Margaret Mary Dillman concurred in that. It was the way she wore her blouses made them think it. You know, a size too small. Growing up, we've all known girls like her. Usually they whistle, too, and they laugh at anything.

Now Roysie was stabbed on his blue velvet sofa. The blood sprayed all over it, Roysie said, like room deodorant. The blood misted his eggshell-white walls. Dappled Tova, the crippled mahogany-coated dachshund Roysie's not supposed to have. The blood ruined his sofa. Morris, Roysie's roommate, neglected to get the sofa cleaned right away, and the stains set. Morris is not the domestic type. Away from the hospital where he works, Morris fancies himself an engineer, a conductor, and is into electric trains. Clever intersecting tracks crisscross their apartment floor, and are what made the assailant stumble and wake up Roysie and slice him like baloney. After Roysie got out of the hospital, he tried Lysol on the blue velvet. What he got was bleached halos around the blood spots. An unbecoming polka dot effect, he says. For Christmas last year. Roysie and Morris bought a Chesterfield divan from Sloan's that's a smash. They pay on it a little a month. Three years it'll take, Roysie says.

The intruder was seen catwalking our building's second-story ledge. In the act of lifting himself over Roysie's window frame, he waved at a couple who remarked him. They were looking for a place to park their red Datsun. The couple identified themselves as Ms. Evangel Cuevas, twenty-three, a flight attendant on her way the next morning to Brazil, and Mr. Pedro García-Rodriquez, twenty-eight, a computer programmer with Apple Electronic, Games Division. They thought, they said, the man probably lived in the apartment he was so unorthodoxly entering and had mistaken them as neighbors he knew. But they were not naive to the ways of New York City. Cuevas and García-Rodriquez talked it over. They decided no harm would be done if the police were told and asked to check. So, after finding a parking space in the next block, Cuevas and García-Rodriquez strolled up to Central

Park West and a police call box there and reported the man to the 20th Precinct. The man, they said, was to all appearances breaking and entering the second-floor front apartment at _____West 7 _____Street.

The police did not come in time to interrupt the burglary or the assault. But the fact that they did come, Detective Sergeant Michael Reardon of the two-oh let me know, got the third charge reduced from murder three to attempted. That's how close Roysie came.

As it was, Roysie was in surgery for two days; five hours immediately after he arrived at Roosevelt emergency and seven hours the next day because the sutures in the bowel leaked after. Overall, Roysie was in the hospital eight weeks.

So Roysie lived and Johnny died.

The night Roysie lived, it was August. The night Johnny died, it was August, too. After the potato harvest. In October, after my sixteenth birthday, I lit out, convinced Margaret Mary Dillman, poor Margaret Mary Dillman, wasn't coming back. Besides me, Margaret Mary was the only one knew the truth. Johnny had been killing her. Punching her baby-full belly. That's why I went for him. Johnny was nothing to me, and I hadn't meant to kill him. Seeing me coming toward him, out of my dress, pale in the taffeta slip, must have frightened him. He fired that little hand pistol he had right at my bosom. Missed by a mile. When I jumped him, he hit me in the eye. And then the world went red, and Johnny was dead. Stabbed with a potato knife.

And one daybreak, in October, I gunned away toward all my tomorrows in a hundred-dollar '49 Hudson I bought from V. V. Wynner. From Jurl back home, I hear V. V. is in jail now. Tax evasion. At the time, V. V. had three used-car lots and a slogan I liked: "I caught you smilin', neighbor." To this day, I think I got a good buy from V. V. Metallic green that Hudson was, with a wasp back and a buzz in its carburetor. And five pretty good tires, which was the important thing. I was traveling alone, and I was going a thousand miles. I piled the rear seat with all I owned and cared about. There was three cardboard suitcases, a box of paperback books, and a Royal portable typewriter. In the front there was only me and $500 cash and a load of to-be-forgottens.

I made it to New York City, to Far Rockaway, Queens, to be exact. I parked that old Hudson in front of a fire hydrant so the city would take care of it for me and walked away from Lyndon, Kay-wy.

Rented a bungalow smack dab on the ocean. The little house stood on stilts about twenty feet from the boardwalk and the high-water mark. The time was after season. The shack was unheated. Winter was coming, and I got her cheap. The landlord's name was Pearlstein, Irving Pearlstein. He was the first Jew I ever met, and I thought his name was magical, an omen that boded well for me. Pearlstein was a hairdresser in Manhattan. He dreamed of going to Hollywood and doing Kim Novak and Arlene Dahl. He said they needed him to become the stars they deserved to be. I hope he got there.

Trying to forget, on weekends I waitressed in a diner. Slinging hash, the pros call it. I called it *reportage*. I met a hairy-chested man. I called it research. He moved in, and I studied him. He kept me warm that winter. He was handy around the house, too.

Trying to remember, weekdays I wrote the novel. My first novel. I called it *Johnny Goodbye*. It was about missing my daddy and loving Malcolm. About Mama and the two old-maid aunts. About Johnny Williams and Margaret Mary Dillman. About Monsignor Roland saying he couldn't remember me coming to his door, late, late, beat up and shot at and begging him to come and save Margaret Mary from her doom. He didn't come. Considering what happened, how could he have forgot?

The lady at Random House was nice. She corrected my grammar. She asked me to write it again, please, changing Monsignor Roland, changing Margaret Mary Dillman. Maybe now, after Roysie, I will.

Personal history, you say. Well, fact and fancy. But if *esthetic distance* is established, individual history becomes *reportage*. It can give you the background and material for a third-person-voice novel. Achieving *esthetic distance* means not taking what happens to you personally, no matter how personal what happens is. *Esthetic distance* objectifies the personal experience. Done right, it makes for unique *reportage*. It makes your fiction read like truth and resonate like art.

If you get too close to your own material, though, you lose perspective. That's what I did the first time I wrote about Johnny. The writing turns *self-indulgent* and sloppy. It gets weepy, drippy, and readers don't like that. Readers don't want to feel worry or happy or excited for writers. They want to be swept away. One way a writer gets them there is by establishing esthetic distance and letting the reader close the gap himself. The reader does that by *identifying*.

If a writer makes it possible for a reader to identify, that writer has succeeded in one basic purpose of storytelling, the *vicarious experience*. A *vicarious experience* is an experience we imagine we have as opposed to one we actually have. A *vicarious experience* is often as satisfying as a real one, and some people prefer them. Most of us like to go where we have never been, especially if it's safe and scarfree. And, no small thing, we can go away and come back without even having to change our clothes. Along the way we may laugh, cry, grow lustful, become excited. We may get an inkling of what it is like to be beautiful, brilliant, privileged, strong, loved. We exercise and entertain the soul through emotions, the mind through ideas, and the body through adventures. After a good read, for a while, the inner beasts quiet down.

A writer is ever after a new story, a fresh experience to give the reader. So when Roysie awoke from the anesthetic, the first thing he saw and the first thing he smelled were the roses I'd sent. And the first thing he found was his favorite thing, a half-pound bar of Hershey's with almonds under his pillow. I'd put it there while he was in the OR. As soon as Roysie was able to talk, while he was still in intensive care, as Roysie's closest living friend, I visited. Heard all about his ordeal, detail by detail, while the terror was strong in him. I met the investigating detective, Sergeant Reardon. Had the man to my apartment for tea. Gave him a book I wrote. Roysie calls my conduct friendship. It was more and less than friendship. You know what it was. It was *reportage*. And I scooped; nobody got Roysie's whole story but me. Not even Sergeant Reardon got as much out of Roysie as I did. So I got a new story, some good new facts, and a new source in Sergeant Reardon. Roysie's misery proved invaluable to me.

Roysie knows the sorry truth. He doesn't mind. Or he forgives me. He says he's looking forward to seeing his story transmogrified and in print. Dear Roysie. He's doing fine now, thank you.

The truth is that the faculty of *reportage* is an artistic flaw. (I call it a flaw because it is not normal and makes living harder.) Somehow, a writer will record, by some means, all the life and people he or she can. That's just how it is. It's tax on the talent, and we all pay.

This strange compulsion, this warp, terrifies some writers. What happens is that one feels insincere at a certain life moment because one is taking note of one's own and/or others' responses so as to be sincere in the amount of fiction. If you're not careful, the flaw can drive you crazy. It's had me in dark water most of my life. André Gide was aghast at himself monitoring the dying of his long-suffering wife, but he couldn't stop. Ernest Hemingway, supposedly self-mocking, did it to himself, in diaries, during his last illness. Anne Frank did it unquestioningly, beautiful doomed child. One way or another the writer does it. We have to.

Reportage is, at best, a filtered truth, a mix of fact and fancy filtered through a writer. It is the truth as perceived, but only more or less and only as long as it makes a good story. The novelist, when the truth gets boring, begins artfully to lie.

As I did, by the way, about Johnny. I made the whole thing up. But you knew that all along. You know I'm too nice a person to have done a thing like that.

Regarding reportage in fiction, I pass along to you some guidelines I use, with the reminder they are, any and all, to be changed as the need arises.

#1. Do anything you have to, excepting detectable crime, for a good story. There is nothing you can do for a great story. Great stories are either lived or dropped in your lap. Great stories are fated. On the other hand, do anything, anything at all, for a great story.

#2. Cultivate people to whom things happen. Pry. Self-important people love it, and most people who are important think they are.

#3. All roads lead to Rome. This means there is no only, or best, way to write. Each of us, all of us, each time, uncovers a way to come to Rome.

#4. Coming to Rome means completing the project, telling the story, writing the novel. It may or may not bring you money, fame, praise, satisfaction, and happiness—all of which are, in the short run, why we do it. In the long run, what is necessary is that each time we come to Rome, we arrive better at our craft. Sometimes it is only by a smidgin. Sometimes it's by a hectare.

#5. It is the nature of truth to become muddy. Move away from the truth as soon as you can into clean and beautiful lies.

#6. Ground your lies in little, verifiable truths. This way you fool most of the people all the time.

#7.   If you want to know something, try living it first or experimenting. If you can't do either, ask an expert. If you can't find an expert, make up whatever you like. No one will publicly gainsay you. Those who know better will be too busy.

#8.   Visualize, visualize. And then write what you see simply and specifically. Avoid simile and metaphor, unless you are seeking effect. Do not seek often or hard for effect.

#9.   For the ring of truth which resonates, throw away most adjectives. Especially "very" and "really" and "super" and such.

#10. In a writer, it is considered a better thing to be amusing than accurate.

And good luck to you.

About the Contributors

FRANKLIN BANDY has had three mystery novels published under the pseudonym Eugene Franklin, and three suspense novels published as paperback originals. His seventh and most recent book, *The Farewell Party* (1980), also a paperback, is a satirical mainstream novel. His last four books were published under his own name. He has also published short stories in the mystery genre and nonfiction articles. He is treasurer of the Mystery Writers of America.

D. R. BENSEN has been an editor for thirty-two years and a writer for the past seven. He recently completed a novella, *Irene, Good Night* (1982), for Targ Editions. He is on the board of the Mystery Writers of America.

BRUCE CASSIDAY wrote radio mysteries for *Suspense* and anthology shows and detective stories for pulp magazines before becoming a magazine editor and novelist. His published books, both fiction and nonfiction, number in the high nineties. Past executive vice president of the Mystery Writers of America, he is general editor of Ungar's *Recognitions* series, mystery section.

THOMAS CHASTAIN's most recent novel is *Nightscape* (1982). His work has appeared on television. An active member of the Mystery Writers of America, he is on the board of directors and was awards chairman the past four years for the annual Edgar banquet.

KEN FOLLETT, born in Wales and now living in England and New York, achieved instant fame with *Eye of the Needle* (1978), a bestseller and a movie, followed by two more bestsellers, *Triple* (1979) and *The Key to Rebecca* (1980). He was a reporter before he started to write novels, and is a recent member of the Mystery Writers of America.

LUCY FREEMAN has written both fiction and nonfiction suspense. Her novel *The Dream* (1971) was adapted for the stage, and her nonfiction book *Betrayal* (1976) appeared as a two-hour film on television. She is past secretary of the board of the Mystery Writers of America and is presently a board member.

EDWARD D. HOCH is a prolific short story writer and novelist. Currently president of the Mystery Writers of America, he is editor of *The Year's Best Mystery and Suspense Stories*.

SHANNON OCORK has been critically admired since the publication in 1980 of *Sports Freak*, her first novel, and the first of the T. T. Baldwin, sports-background mystery series. A former photographer, she now writes full time. She is a member of the Mystery Writers of America.

ELEANOR SULLIVAN is editor of *Ellery Queen's Mystery Magazine* and author of short stories and film scripts. Her short story "Something Like Growing Pains" appeared in the MWA anthology *Killers of the Mind*, published in 1974. She is a member of the board of directors of the Mystery Writers of America and a past secretary.

HILLARY WAUGH is a past president of the Mystery Writers of America and the author of forty mystery novels, including *Madman at My Door* (1978), *The Young Prey* (1969), and *Last Seen Wearing* . . . (1952) which was listed by the *London Times* as one of the one hundred best mysteries ever written. He was named a Grand Master by the Swedish Academy of Detection in 1981.

HELEN WELLS's Cherry Ames nurse books and Vicki Barr flight stewardess stories continue to sell well in fifteen countries including the United States and Canada. They have been optioned for films and television. She has written many adult short stories, some broadcast on radio, and novels for teenagers and younger readers, most of them mysteries, as well as three historical novels for young readers that are used as textbooks in schools. She is a member of the Mystery Writers of America, serving four terms on the board of directors, and of the Authors Guild of America.